WHITE HOUSE INTERPRETER

THE ART OF INTERPRETATION

Harry Obst

authorHOUSE®

AuthorHouse™
1663 Liberty Drive
Bloomington, IN 47403
www.authorhouse.com
Phone: 1-800-839-8640

First published by AuthorHouse 4/12/2010

ISBN: 978-1-4520-0616-1 (e)
ISBN: 978-1-4520-0615-4 (sc)
ISBN: 978-1-4520-0614-7 (hc)

Library of Congress Control Number: 2010904282

Printed in the United States of America
Bloomington, Indiana

This book is printed on acid-free paper.

CONTENTS

ACKNOWLEDGEMENTS

First and foremost, I am deeply grateful to my friend Robert E. Field of Pennsylvania. Without his motivational prodding, generous support, caustic but productive criticism, and his conviction that this book was needed to fill a long-existing gap, it might never have been completed.

Next, I wish to thank my wife Elnina, who keeps an orderly and clean house, for putting up with endless months of boxes, piles of papers, and books cluttering up the family environment.

I owe thanks to several colleagues and friends who volunteered to read a chapter or two and helped to weed out my mistakes.

My gratitude also reaches back to several presidents and their assistants, from Lyndon Johnson to George Herbert Walker Bush, who have graciously provided me with copies of official photographs, some of which help to illustrate this book.

Finally, I wish to salute the interpreters and translators of the Office of Language Services of the Department of State in Washington, an office that I had the privilege of heading from 1984 to 1997. Frequently understaffed and underfunded, and often underappreciated, they have served the White House, the cabinet officers, and the leaders of Congress with outstanding professional skills, deep patriotic loyalty, and tireless and unselfish devotion.

INTRODUCTION

Between November of 1985 and May of 1988, one of the most important series of discussions between two men in all of human history took place. At stake were hundreds of billions of dollars and the fate of hundreds of millions of people. The success or failure of these talks would dramatically shape or change the future of many countries in the 1990s and well into the third millennium. Those countries included the two mightiest on the globe, the Soviet Union and the United States of America, as well as some of the smallest, which had yearned for decades to regain their freedom of thought and action, such as Estonia, Latvia, Lithuania, Romania, and Uzbekistan.

The talks between two former archenemies were difficult, overshadowed by mutual distrust and suspicion, jeopardized by occasional outbursts of anger and surges of impatience. On those turbulent waves of suspicions and frequent misunderstandings of each other's true motives, of general overtures, specific suggestions, and calculated probes rode the fragile ship of mutual hope and basic goodwill that had brought the two leaders together in the first place. One, a courageous revolutionary with a sparkling intellect, the other a conservative, patriotic, and idealistic American who was tormented by the specter of a possible nuclear war, but who also understood that now there existed an opportunity to end the cold war that was likely to precipitate that catastrophe.

Every hour of their private discussions was weighty and precarious. Many a sentence spoken in those meetings was of great consequence. Most people would believe that Ronald Reagan was listening and speaking to Mikhail Gorbachev and vice versa. But that was not the case.

In most meetings, Gorbachev was speaking to Pavel Palazchenko and listening carefully to Dimitry Zarechnak. And Reagan did not hear the Soviet arguments and entreaties as presented by Gorbachev, because he did not speak any Russian. Every phrase came to him as it was fashioned and presented by Palazchenko. Every time he wanted to make a point to Gorbachev, he had to make that point to Zarechnak, who had to analyze his spoken words and gestures carefully to divine the true underlying meaning before he could make the equivalent argument in Russian to the Soviet leader.

The success or failure of these private meetings did not just rest on the shoulders of the two principal interlocutors. They rested in large measure on the analytical abilities, intellectual acumen, communication skills, and emotional stability of the only two people the leaders could fully understand—their professional interpreters.

Few people, especially in the United States, understand the profession of interpretation.

They know what lawyers, engineers, architects, and brain surgeons are all about. But the art of interpretation is a mystery to many. They may assume that it consists of bilingual people changing words spoken in one language into the same words of another language. That is not at all what professional interpretation is. In challenging situations, accurate interpretation is no less sophisticated, complex, and intellectually demanding than brain surgery. The professional interpreter is required to carry more general knowledge into each job than architects and engineers need in the daily exercise of their profession. It requires the analytical skills of trial lawyers and their acting ability in the courtroom. It also requires a great deal of creativity. It is a true profession in the academic sense of the word, but American universities have not bothered to seriously analyze it and embrace it. As a result, they neither understand it nor offer it a home alongside other professions of equal value for the welfare of their country.

The first object of this book is to explain to the reader what the art of interpretation is and what it covers, from diplomatic interpreting to practicing the profession in the courtroom, hospital, the European Union, on live television, or escorting foreign visitors on long study tours.

The second purpose is to sound a trumpet call for long overdue action in overhauling this profession in the United States. There are more high-quality interpreting schools at the academic institutions of tiny Finland than in all of the universities of the United States combined.

Our ignorance and neglect of the professions of interpretation and translation is costing the United States hundreds of billions of lost export earnings each year and thousands of American and foreign lives lost in the wars that we are drawn into. There is much other damage done to our society because of this neglect: letting criminals go free and innocents go to jail because of faulty interpretation, depriving foreign visitors or speakers of other languages of proper medical care in our hospitals and doctor's offices, and even exonerating wife beaters while deporting their battered spouses.

The book is designed to stay away from theory while it enlightens you. It is not written for the American academic community, where virtually nobody has been listening for over a hundred years anyhow. Nowhere is the ignorance about professional interpretation greater than at our universities, which are preoccupied with the teaching of theoretical linguistics, a discipline of little value to society when compared with the many benefits derived from applied language training. Nowhere is the profession more neglected. Therefore, this book is written for the average reader in language everybody can understand. It uses a minimum of linguistic terminology.

If the current sad state of the profession is ever to improve in the United States, interested groups from outside academia will have to take action. And they might do that once they understand what is at stake for them and the country. It is also written for the American business community. The absence of well-trained and reliable interpreters is costing our economy not only hundreds of billions in lost export earnings but also many millions in other economic damage. Once businesses understand this, they may be willing to motivate American universities to provide the interpreter and translator training that the American economy and society need. The federal government and interpretation experts have urged the universities to provide this training for decades and never gotten a meaningful response. The day that the American business community demands such training, academia may finally listen. Successful bold initiatives in this country usually come from the private sector.

This book is written by a professional interpreter who knows the profession from working in the trenches (courts, escort trips, military missions) and from interpreting for seven American presidents. It is written by an author who for thirteen years was the director of the Office of Language Services at the U.S. Department of State in Washington (more than one thousand contract and staff interpreters work for this office). It is written by a person who ran an interpreting school for seven years and who was its principal instructor.

This is not a book of theories. It is a book based on reality and empirical knowledge. It is written to entertain you while it informs you. I include five chapters on my work with American presidents, looking at them from the interpreter's perspective inside the Oval Office and elsewhere. It gives you a feel for the daily experiences of interpreters by recounting challenging, highly satisfying, and very disappointing days. It also includes a few bizarre or amusing anecdotes that my friends have urged me to write down on paper, so others might enjoy them. The occasional levity is designed to keep your interest while the book endeavors to guide you, step by step, to a thorough understanding of the art of interpretation, an important profession in any civilized and developed society, especially in the United States of America, which has turned its back on it for so long.

PRESIDENTIAL VIGNETTES

LYNDON B. JOHNSON

1963–1969

DINNER AT BLAIR HOUSE

It was not at 1600 but at 1651 Pennsylvania Avenue, diagonally across from the White House, where I met my first president. A working dinner at Blair House on June 3, 1965, was to kick off a visit by German Chancellor Ludwig Erhard. Blair House, where General Robert E. Lee once declined Lincoln's offer to lead the Union Army in the Civil War, had been a government guesthouse since World War II.

I had been on a long escort assignment with a German newspaper editor since April 26 and had reached Denver on May 29 when the phone in my hotel room rang late in the evening. It was Donald Barnes, the chief interpreter. He ordered me back to Washington the next morning, because Erhard was to come there on short notice to see President Johnson. "Good!" I said. "You want me to observe how such a visit is interpreted."

"Observe?" Barnes exclaimed. "Have you read your job description?"

Although I had been hired as the then only German staff interpreter about five months earlier and had gone through several weeks of in-house training, I was not ready for such a difficult assignment at the highest level. In fact, I had requested the assignment with the editor of a small newspaper in order to practice my consecutive notes and ideograms. They left a lot to be desired. The journalist liked to make lively and humorous speeches at Rotary Clubs and other local gatherings. This gave me an opportunity to try different techniques without having to worry that my mistakes would cause problems in international relations.

Back in Washington the next day, I was nervous and worried. The chancellor was coming with two interpreters of his own. One of them was Heinz Weber, probably the best German-English interpreter in the world at that time (maybe at any time). The other was Hermann Küsterer, another seasoned professional. Would it not be like a young tenor stepping on the stage next to Luciano Pavarotti and Placido Domingo? How could I possibly get through this without suffering major embarrassment?

Fortunately, there were many veteran interpreters on the State Department staff. I asked some of them for helpful hints on what to do and not to do. I spoke with Charles Sedgwick, one of my trainers, who had accompanied President Kennedy to Paris, with James Wickel, then the senior interpreter for Japanese, and with Bill Krimer, the senior interpreter for Russian.

Their first advice was to buy myself a dark-blue pinstriped suit. Diplomatic protocol expected and often demanded that interpreters wear such standard diplomatic attire when interpreting in public or at dinners. Staff interpreters did not get a clothing allowance. We had to buy our own business attire, including tuxedos, with our private funds. Bill Krimer told me to use a narrow interpreting notebook that could quickly be slipped into a jacket pocket to disappear during photo ops. Jim Wickel told me not to be afraid of presidents but to beware of their mid-level aides and of the Secret Service agents, who inadvertently will push interpreters away from the principals and out of earshot. Charles Sedgwick, a Harvard PhD and former Broadway and Hollywood actor, told me to eat a sandwich before dinner. "You may be served," he said, "but do not expect to get a chance to eat." Charles, a martini drinker when not interpreting, also gave me advice on the consumption of alcohol. "You will probably be scared the first time out, but do not try to calm your nerves with anything strong. You may take a glass of sherry or half a glass of wine, if offered. But even one full glass of wine may impair your ability to properly analyze information and pick up nuances or between-the-lines messages."

When my taxi pulled up at Blair House in the pouring rain, all of this advice was still stored in my mind, but I was frightened and my heart was pounding. Two Secret Service agents checked my credentials and let me proceed to the door. I rang the doorbell. When the door opened, I was greeted by an elderly gentleman who seemed the spitting image of a London butler. "Good evening, sir!" he said with a warm smile and took my raincoat. "You are the first to arrive. I would suggest that you take a seat in the parlor. May I offer you a sherry?"

"Yes, a dry sherry, please," I answered nervously.

The parlor walls were lined with American historical oil paintings. Too agitated to sit down, I walked around the room from painting to painting, trying in vain to slow down my heartbeat.

The doorbell rang again. It was Dean Rusk, also in a raincoat, also asking for a dry sherry. I turned to face him as he entered the parlor, glass in hand. He did not know who I was. Being the consummate diplomat, he bowed slightly and said, "I am Dean Rusk, the secretary of state."

I returned the bow. "I am Harry Obst, the American interpreter."

A puzzled look replaced his smile. "I have never seen you before. Where do you work?"

"I am a staff interpreter at the State Department."

"Really? How long have you been with us?"

"Five months, Mr. Secretary."

And then came the question that would haunt me for many years.

"How long have you been interpreting, then?"

"Just five months, sir."

His mouth opened slightly, not to sip his sherry, but in disbelief. He did not ask any more questions. But in his mind he must have made a checkmark. "A totally inexperienced interpreter! I better watch him like a hawk." And that he did from that day on, examining every word I uttered in his presence with a critical magnifying glass. Nobody else ever doubted my translations as much. Nobody else corrected them as often as he did. As his knowledge of German was limited, many corrections were unwarranted. But I quickly learned that a diplomatic interpreter does not complain when unjustly corrected. You also apologize for the mistakes that you did not make.

Obst forming the language bridge between Chancellor Erhard and President Johnson. *White House photo*

Next I greeted Ludwig Erhard, Gerhard Schröder, and Heinz Weber when the German party arrived. I had first met Erhard in Bonn when I was a student at the Germersheim campus of Mainz University, the home of its school for professional interpreters and translators. Even though it is one of the best university schools in Europe for learning professional interpretation, I was not interested in becoming an interpreter at that time. I elected to take courses in translation of the written word instead and later graduated as a translator. Nevertheless, I was asked one day to travel to the German Bundestag in Bonn with a handful of my fellow students to assist German congressmen with interpreting. This was in 1955, and I was assigned to Erhard. He was then minister of economics in Chancellor Konrad Adenauer's cabinet as well as a Bundestag deputy (the German system did not mandate a separation of powers). Ten years had passed since. Erhard did not remember me, nor did I mention our previous encounter.

Gerhard Schröder, a namesake of the later German chancellor from the other big party, was foreign minister at the time. Heinz Weber was the typical Rhinelander, courteous and laid back. Nothing ever fazed him. He greeted me with a smile and did not look down his nose at a mere rookie, knowing from the day before, when we had interpreted for Secretary of Defense Robert McNamara, that I still had a lot to learn.

Before the president arrived, the butler explained to me that the two interpreters would sit at the ends of the table and the four principals would be facing each other in the middle, to ease the flow of the conversation. He pointed to my chair and remarked that Charles De Gaulle and Winston Churchill had sat in it. This did not make me any less nervous.

Once LBJ arrived, the dinner got under way. There was a little small talk, and we got into substantive discussions rather quickly. The topics, mostly economic and military, were familiar to me from having read the State Department briefing book for the Erhard visit.

I had seen Johnson often on television and had noticed that the role of president fit him naturally. He had always wanted to be top dog in any environment anyhow. As a result, he felt completely at home in that role, similar to Eisenhower, Kennedy, and even Bill Clinton, despite the latter's informal way of being natural. Diametrical opposites would be Nixon and George W. Bush (for whom I have never interpreted). They always seemed to try hard to look presidential and walk upright and somewhat stiffly, jutting out their chins, emanating an air of artificiality. With LBJ, I always felt that if he had been in a crowd of a hundred Washington politicians when a spaceship from another planet landed unexpectedly in the nation's capital, the captain of that ship would have made a beeline for him, not needing to say to anybody, "Take me to your leader!"

You could not help but be awed by his physical presence. Everything about him was big, his Texas-sized frame, his hands, even his ears. This evening he was relaxed and smiling. There were only six of us, and the food and wine were excellent. My fear began to dissipate a little because the president treated me the same as Weber, whom he knew from previous encounters.

But it was not only Johnson I was awed by. Heinz Weber's English renditions flowed like a river on a sunny day. He delivered them seemingly effortlessly. I did not discover any mistakes or omissions. He also used a small pad that he carried in his jacket pocket. By contrast, I occasionally had trouble reading my notes or my memory and made several minor mistakes. Weber noticed them but never corrected me. He taught me a valuable lesson immediately. You do not correct minor mistakes of your colleague unless they damage the substance of the conversation. Usually, nobody but the other interpreter notices them anyhow. Do not sweat the small stuff. There are enough big problems to solve to achieve accurate interpretation.

I sneaked a couple of sips from my wineglass while Weber was talking. What a great wine!

Wistfully, I stared at the glass and at the meat on my plate while the interpreting work went on nonstop. It was my first whiff of the perennial torture interpreters suffer at banquets and meals. You can look and smell, but you rarely can touch.

I somehow got through the evening without embarrassment, but a tough agenda was waiting in the morning. When the president left, he shook my hand like everybody else's. His hand was big and his grip firm. A hundred of his handshakes were ahead of me. The Germans had a limousine waiting and left in a hurry, giving me no chance to consult with Weber. The butler handed me my raincoat, and I walked to Seventeenth and Pennsylvania, where I hailed a cab to go back to the State Department. Later I drove home through the rain with a little more confidence. But I did not sleep well that night.

THE OVAL OFFICE

The next morning, somewhat pale and still apprehensive, I took the elevator up to the seventh floor of the Department of State. The main building is arranged like a hierarchical pyramid. The higher up your office, the more important your function. The seventh floor houses the offices of the secretary and his most important assistants, while the eighth and topmost floor holds the fabulously appointed reception rooms of the department, in Washington only rivaled by some of the rooms in the White House.

Another baptism of fire awaited me here, my first plunge into serious simultaneous interpretation. Most of my training had been in consecutive interpretation, working from memory and notes with ample time for analysis of the message hidden behind the spoken words. Working in simultaneous, from memory only, just three to five words behind the speaker, affords too little time for reliable analysis. It is hard for accomplished interpreters and murder for a mere beginner, as I was that day.

We had assembled in what was then known as the Undersecretary's Conference Room. The room had two positions for simultaneous interpreters behind a wall with a window looking into the conference room. We each had a microphone and earphones. The conference participants were listening to us through their own earphones. It is important for interpreters to be able to see the speakers in order to be able to read their gestures and other body language, tell who is speaking, watch the passing around of documents, and see what places are pointed to on wall maps, projected slides, or charts.

The principal briefer was Secretary of Defense McNamara. He was known to be a fast and rambling speaker. Even more annoying to Weber and me was the subject: nuclear missiles in Europe, an overview of the arsenals of NATO and the Warsaw Pact. Terms like "MIRVs" (multiple, independently targeted reentry vehicles) and "phased-array radar" were thrown at us in bundles, together with a shower of numbers. Erhard was half lulled to sleep by this rapid-fire technical onslaught, while his foreign minister listened attentively.

I was struggling through the entire briefing, using up buckets of adrenalin. My only comfort was that Weber, too, was straining when it was his turn, proving how daunting was the task in front of us. When the one-hour briefing was over, both of us had exhausted much of our mental energy. For me, there was no time to rest. Next on the schedule was the Oval Office, where Weber would be replaced by his colleague Hermann Küsterer.

We went straight down to the main entrance of the building and left in separate motorcades, the Americans first, the Germans a little later, so that the chancellor could make an appropriate entrance before the press and be properly greeted on arrival. In each motorcade, there were security cars with blaring sirens and flashing blue lights. That detail was from the State Department, not from the Secret Service. In front of all this were outriders from the District of Columbia police on motorcycles, clearing the way and blocking the traffic on side streets until we had passed.

Thank God, this was only a working visit, sparing us interpreters at least the elaborate arrival ceremony on the South Lawn, accorded during official and state visits, with anthems, review of the troops, and speeches on live television.

Before I had time to compose my nerves, I found myself, for the first time, in the Oval Office for a one-on-one between the two leaders. At least Dean Rusk was not there to watch my every word. Still, I felt insecure and worried. During the opening exchange of small talk, I let Küsterer do the interpreting in both directions while I stayed a step back. I looked around the room. It was not opulently furnished under Johnson. It had three comforting features: a fireplace, a tall grandfather clock that reminded me of several such clocks dispersed over my grandfather's apartment in East Prussia's capital of Königsberg, and an enormous lounge chair for the president. Still, my heart was not slowing down. LBJ plopped himself into his chair. Erhard took a smaller armchair across from him, his famous cigar in his left hand. Hermann and I pulled up chairs and whipped our notebooks out of our coat pockets.

I did not react fast enough to interpret Johnson's opening statement. Küsterer had to do it for me. Suddenly, I realized that if I did not take over the next time the president spoke, my interpreting career would be over. When LBJ made his next statement, Küsterer smiled at me and made a hand gesture indicating that it was my turn. The first of thousands of sentences I was to interpret at the Oval Office over the next thirty years finally rolled off my tongue.

The usual procedure in a private meeting between two leaders is that each interpreter does his own principal into the other language whenever possible. The reasons for this are many. The local interpreter usually will have read the same briefing book as his principal, having familiarized himself beforehand with the subjects, proper names, and places that are likely to come up in the conservation. He will know the current policy of his government. He will know what just happened in his country: a surprise resolution in the Congress, the resignation of a cabinet member yesterday, and so on.

Even more important is that he will be more familiar with the cultural and regional peculiarities of his country than the visiting interpreter. In the 1960s, no European interpreter could have guessed the meaning of "I think it is time to punt." American football was not yet known in Europe. Conversely, an American interpreter might have been baffled by the statement "And all of this happened in the eighty-ninth minute!" not knowing that soccer games last ninety minutes.

Same w/ idioms

Reagan once said, "When it comes to weapons systems, I am from Missouri." A European interpreter may have had a hard time interpreting this as "When it comes to weapons systems, you will have to prove it to me first." A literal translation would not have made any sense to most foreign leaders. They might have assumed a literal translation to mean "When it comes to weapons systems, I am as ignorant as a farmer from Missouri."

Interpreting has little to do with transferring words to another language. It is all about accurately capturing messages. Even more so than the always reliable Küsterer, Heinz Weber was not only a master in correctly analyzing messages, he sometimes was a magician when it came to finding the most suitable formulation in the other language. From our first encounter on, he became the yardstick by which I measured my own progress in gradually mastering the art of diplomatic interpretation.

Something else I learned this first day at the Oval Office was that Johnson had a great deal of admiration for Erhard's economic policies and for the chancellor's ideas for transforming German postwar society. Erhard had dubbed the social component of his policies *Die Formierte Gesellschaft* (the Shaped Society). Some of these ideas were echoed in LBJ's "Great Society." Educating and training the disadvantaged, creating jobs, and in the process, lifting more people out of poverty into the middle class were projects dear to the heart of both leaders.

"One-on-One" in the Oval Office. From left: German
interpreter Heinz Weber, Chancellor Ludwig Erhard, Harry
Obst, President Lyndon Johnson. *White House photo*

RIGHT EAR—LEFT EAR

*Similar issues in
ASL dealings w/
background*

One peculiar problem interpreters faced when dealing with Johnson and
Erhard was that both were hard of hearing in the left ear, in the case
of Erhard, the result of a war injury. This could be solved to a degree
by each interpreter positioning himself close to the right ear of the
person to whom he was speaking. However, this meant that you were
close to the bad ear of your own principal, making it hard to whisper
information to each other when a private consultation was needed. At
formal events, a state dinner, for instance, the interpreter is normally

seated to the left of the principal, leaving the right side—the place of honor—to a high-ranking official or special guest. As a consequence, you get stuck with a bad ear in a situation where there are many other sounds in the room: the conversations of other guests and the noises produced by the china, glasses, and silverware being banged around by the diners and waiters.

If only one interpreter is handling an informal meeting between two clients hard of hearing in the same ear, this can become a major challenge. There is no geometrical seating arrangement in which the two clients can look at each other that gives the interpreter two good ears. As a result, you constantly have to speak in a normal voice to one person and sort of holler into the ear of the other. If you ever mix up the two ears, you will get an unpleasant reaction from both sides. One will tell you to keep your voice down, the other that he could not understand anything. Erhard would complain politely, but Johnson would bawl you out. He always demanded perfection from all his assistants. On the other hand, if you had done a good job, LBJ would virtually never fail to thank you personally. I received more warm words, courtesy photographs, and personal attention from him than from any other president I worked for.

FLIGHT TO CAPE CANAVERAL

In September 1966, Erhard was back in Washington. The National Aeronautics and Space Administration, then headed by James Webb, was in the midst of its Gemini flights in preparation for the moon landing ordered by President Kennedy to be accomplished by the end of the decade. The political discussion in the Oval Office on German military offset payments—the most unpleasant encounter between Johnson and Erhard that I ever interpreted—had not gone well. Maybe as a gesture to mollify the distraught German chancellor, LBJ suggested that the two of them go down to the Kennedy Space Center at Cape Canaveral in Florida on September 27 to get an on-site briefing on the space program. We boarded *Air Force One* at Andrews Air Force Base, where the presidential air fleet is stationed, jetted south, and landed directly on the Kennedy Space Center airstrip.

At the Cape, we received briefings by Gemini astronaut James Lovell and by Dr. Kurt Debus. Debus and Wernher von Braun were the two crown jewels of the 120-person German rocket development team that had been seized and transported to the United States after the German World War II surrender. In 1966, von Braun was director of the Marshall Space Flight Center in Huntsville, Alabama. Debus was director of the Kennedy Space Center at Cape Canaveral. Von Braun designed and built the moon rockets and shipped them via the Tennessee and Mississippi rivers and through the Gulf of Mexico to Debus, whose job it was to launch them into space from Florida.

Erhard's mood was boosted a little by this visit. He and LBJ climbed a podium in front of a giant Saturn V rocket to address the employees of the center. The chancellor voiced his respect and admiration in a courteous, brief speech that I whispered into the right ear of the president while Erhard's interpreter put it into English from consecutive notes minutes later. Why two interpretations of the same message? The instant whispering of the first interpreter allows the listening leader to react with smiles, nods, and other body language at the exact point when it is called for. The whispering interpreter, only a few seconds behind the speaker, is usually uncomfortable with this arrangement. He has to interpret without sufficient time for analysis and for finding the most suitable formulations in the target language. The second interpreter has a few minutes for the same task. He will always be more accurate and more elegant in his phrasing, showing up the performance of his colleague, whose principal may wonder why he is better than his own interpreter.

President Johnson had given up most of his day for this spontaneous trip to Florida. Part of that day had previously been scheduled for other activities, among them a discussion of the situation in Vietnam with Secretary of Defense Robert McNamara and other top advisers on the war. LBJ simply had all of them put on the airplane to have that discussion and transact some other business of the day in flight. While he had given Erhard a lot of time on the flight south, he now needed time for this during the two-hour return trip.

He instructed James Webb, who also was along for the trip, to keep Erhard busy with a briefing on the planned future of American space travel. This included plans to train astronauts from other nations to occasionally accompany Americans into space. Webb, who always loved to talk, threw himself into this task with gusto. Erhard, who had just endured two briefings at Cape Canaveral, lit a cigar. His body language told me that he was not really interested in another space briefing and was somewhat put off that LBJ was holding a staff discussion while he was on board. As Webb fired away at a rapid clip, I took fewer notes than usual, knowing that I would do the chancellor a favor by leaving out a lot of redundancies and technical detail. Every four minutes or so, I gave the chancellor a summary of the main points, leaving out what I knew would not interest him much. I hoped that Webb knew no German, in contrast to Secretary Rusk, so that my little game would not get discovered.

ethical correct?
As interpreters, shouldn't we
interpret everything. NOT summarize in our own words

When the briefing was over, Webb took me aside and asked to look at my notes, just a few circles, squares, arrows, and word abbreviations on each page. "I admired your translation," he complimented me. "You got every little detail across, just the way I said it. But I am even more intrigued by your notes. You have only two or three notations for each long sentence. How can so few notes capture so much detail?"

I was relieved to learn that he had not caught on to what I had done and explained how interpreting notes work in interplay with short-term memory. He asked me to call him in Washington because he wanted me to teach this kind of note-taking to his immediate staff. I never took him up on that. Thankfully, he never called me back on this proposal.

The fasten-seat-belts sign came on. We seemed to be approaching Andrews Air Force Base. The president swiveled his big chair around and started to talk to Erhard again. I unbuckled and left my seat against the wall, kneeling down on the floor between the two, so as to not block their view of each other. I was not worried about the landing. The traffic gets cleared out in front of the president's plane, and you usually land like a feather. A few minutes earlier, I had noticed that LBJ was having a whispering exchange with Press Secretary Bill Moyers. The only words I had overheard were "Baltimore" and "Philadelphia." It meant nothing to me. Suddenly, in the middle of a sentence I was interpreting, the plane hit something with a big thud. It jarred me so hard that I thought my teeth were falling out. Even super-tough LBJ straightened up in his chair and looked alarmed. Then I heard the four engines reverse and tires screech. We were on the ground somewhere. The fog outside was so dense that you could not see twenty feet.

When I finally got out of the plane and went into the building, I was amazed to see that we were at National Airport. How was that possible? No four-engine jets were allowed to land there. The runways were much too short for a Boeing 707. Later, I found out what had happened. Twenty minutes or so out of Washington, Moyers had told the president that Andrews, Dulles Airport, and Baltimore-Washington Airport were closed because of heavy fog. The crew wanted to divert to Philadelphia. LBJ did not want to go to Philadelphia. He wanted to land near Washington, if there was any way to do so. Texans will take risks that others might avoid.

The captain called into the approach control of National Airport. That smaller airport was also completely closed to all traffic, but there was a small hole in the fog at the north end of the runway, reported the tower. Knowing he had very little runway to work with and no headwind, the captain maneuvered *Air Force One* through that hole in the fog and dropped the plane straight down like a ton of bricks over the north end of the runway. It was the hardest landing I ever made on any plane, and I have made over 1,300 landings at airports.

FIDDLING WHILE WASHINGTON IS BURNING

Shortly after the tragic assassination of Martin Luther King, Jr. in Memphis, riots broke out in Washington. On April 10, 1968, the city was still in turmoil. That was the day when Austrian Chancellor Joseph Klaus was in Washington during an extended visit to the United States. In the morning, LBJ and the chancellor had a one-on-one meeting in the Oval Office, for which I was the only interpreter. A festive banquet had been arranged for the evening. The Austrian interpreter who had been scheduled to accompany his chancellor had fallen ill, as had my only backup, William Krimer, the senior staff interpreter for Russian, whose German was still adequate in the 1960s. He had gone to high school in Berlin, where his family had fled after the Soviet Revolution of 1917, before later moving on to London and eventually New York. This left me to cover the entire trip alone. Chicago, San Francisco, and Los Angeles remained on the itinerary after Washington.

I had heard on the morning news that rioting and looting was under way on Seventh Street and Fourteenth Street in the District. During the lunch period, the chancellor was busy with his embassy. That gave me an opportunity to jump in my car and drive out to near Seventh Street, during that year a busy commercial strip with many stores for blocks, all the way down to Pennsylvania Avenue. When I got there, I found the street lined with many police and heavily armed soldiers of the National Guard. Store windows were bashed in; several fires were burning; scores of black youths and men carried furniture, television sets, and other loot out of the stores without being stopped by the police or the soldiers. LBJ had given orders not to use any force. "Things can be replaced, people cannot" was a quote attributed to him in the newspapers the next day.

The president, his soul weighted down with King's murder, losses in Vietnam, and the riots in several cities, did his best to make the day enjoyable for Klaus. The Oval Office talk in the morning had been pleasant for the most part, and an elaborate state dinner with a touch of Vienna awaited the Austrian leader in the evening when he returned to a nervous and beleaguered White House.

While streets in Washington were still burning, a state of emergency had been declared and an evening curfew imposed; strolling violins from the Marine Corps Band moved from table to table in their resplendent dress uniforms, serenading the guests with Strauss waltzes. Wine glasses and festive bouquets were mirrored in the White House china, men talked about their trips to Salzburg and Vienna, while their ladies in their best evening gowns threw flirtatious glances at the musicians. It reminded me of Emperor Nero playing his violin while Rome was burning.

Interpreting the toasts and after-dinner entertainment in the East Room kept me busy until 11:00 pm, when the chief of protocol, Ambassador Duke, came to speak to me. For the first time, I learned from him that there was a state of emergency and a curfew out there. His dilemma was that he had run out of rooms at a secure hotel and at Blair House, where the dinner guests were to be put up for the night. I was stranded with no way to get home to our house in Virginia. We were having this conversation behind the backs of LBJ and Ladybird Johnson. Duke warned me that driving my car through the District was too dangerous. I was certain to get arrested.

The president overheard this conversation, turned around, and said, "Duke, give him my limo to take him home!" Nobody argues with the president. Ten minutes later, the Lincoln Continental pulled up in the driveway on the North side.

SOMEBODY STOLE THE PRESIDENT'S CAR

The driver, a slim, tall black man wearing his chauffeur's cap and white gloves, looked at me disdainfully. Driving an interpreter home on a night like this, without a Secret Service escort, was not what he had expected. His off-putting manner made me get into the back of the limousine. He opened the door reluctantly with a slight scowl on his face. I told him to go across the Roosevelt Bridge and pick up the George Washington Parkway.

For a moment, I enjoyed the experience, leaning back in the comfortable seat. I hoped somebody would still be up at home to see me arrive in the president's limousine. But that moment of joy would not last long. When we arrived at the bridge, it was blocked and patrolled by the National Guard. A huge black sergeant and another soldier ordered us to stop.

The sergeant held a flashlight and pointed it at the side of the Lincoln. There was a painted seal on it reading "The President of the United States." Because of the tinted windows, he could not make out who was inside. But he knew that the president would not go anywhere, even in the dead of night, without a Secret Service escort. Conclusion: somebody had stolen the president's car. This riot was certainly getting out of hand.

The driver and I were ordered out at gunpoint and had to spread-eagle against the car. The soldier patted us down for weapons. When it was clear that we were unarmed, we were allowed to turn around and tell the sergeant why we were on the road. I was in my tuxedo and did not look much like a car thief. Did the driver wear white gloves not to leave any fingerprints? The sergeant's eyes scanned us suspiciously. He took his time examining our government credentials. My State Department card did not impress him, but the driver had a White House pass. I conjured up my best diplomatic skills to talk him into letting us across the bridge. Finally, he relented, but not without a parting shot. As he handed me back my badge, he looked me sternly in the eyes and barked, "I could have shot you dead, and I would have gotten away with it. You are in violation of a strict curfew. Now get yourself home and stay in your house!"

It was not the glorious ride home I had hoped for. Worse, by the time I got there, nobody was up to witness my arrival. What a downer!

ONE HUNDRED DECISIONS IN BED

President Johnson had a soft spot in his heart for interpreters because he understood how fiendishly difficult high-level interpreting often is and how much knowledge good interpreters possess and must keep storing in their heads in order to remain at the top of their profession. He would not hesitate to ask interpreters for advice, especially on the character and modus operandi of foreign leaders. Few presidents ever did that. LBJ realized that veteran interpreters, having worked for previous administrations, had repeatedly sat in on confidential meetings with durable politicians like De Gaulle, Andrei Gromyko, Marshal Tito, and others. They had gained certain knowledge and experience that few of his regular advisers could command. He also had great respect for people who could effortlessly handle two or more languages. He knew from his own efforts of trying to understand and speak Spanish what an enormous effort is needed to reach native fluency in another language, something he never fully accomplished.

Chief Interpreter Donald Barnes once told a story at a staff meeting that reflects LBJ's respect for diplomatic interpreters. A foreign labor leader asked the president what he would do if his entire cabinet went on strike and did not show up for work. LBJ responded with a grin that this would not be a problem. He would temporarily appoint interpreters to run each department.

"These guys and gals have enough general knowledge in their heads and have enough smarts that they could hold down any secretary's job for about a month without embarrassing me. After a month, though, they would run out of ammunition. But by then, I would have settled the strike."

My quote here is a paraphrase, but very close to what Don, who interpreted at that labor leader meeting, actually told us. Even though this was undoubtedly a tongue-in-cheek remark, it reflected his grasp of what high-level interpreting entails.

This anecdote speaks to the essential difference between translators and interpreters. Translators have all kinds of external help for accurately transferring the messages contained in a written text into another language: dictionaries, specialized glossaries, reference works, telephone calls to experts or experienced colleagues, searches on the Internet, and other means. With very few exceptions, interpreters have only one source to consult: the knowledge stored in their heads. Their knowledge about the subject at hand, and the range of terminology in their working languages residing in their brain, will make or break them. That is why all professional interpreters are such curious people with so many interests, always trying to keep up with the latest developments in the most important fields. You will rarely have a boring conversation with an experienced interpreter. They can cover the waterfront and thread their way through the rarely visited desert.

However, it is rare that an interpreter has a private conversation with a sitting president. Reagan's handlers forbade us outright to ever speak to the president privately. We were only to answer questions that the president might ask us directly. Few of us veterans paid any attention to these tunnel-vision instructions. When the president found himself in a dilemma, we would whisper unsolicited advice into his ear. Why should we have our president or our country embarrassed when we could steer him out of the fog with just a word or two? This was not such a rare happening in the second Reagan administration, when the president occasionally would have trouble hearing or concentrating properly. In a few instances, he would either not understand the thrust of a question or be at a loss for an appropriate answer. Reagan always was grateful for the assistance and generally was very approachable and kind.

Private conversations with Johnson were not so rare, as several of my colleagues had told me. Once, a German visitor was late arriving at the White House. LBJ was sitting on a balcony bench, looking south toward the river, as I stepped in front of him to report my arrival. He did not return my greeting, but bawled me out: "Mr. Interpreter [he rarely called me by my name], you are blocking my view of the Jefferson Memorial!" I apologized and took one step to the left. He grinned and said that each day was so busy that having a few minutes to look out at a peaceful scene was a great boon to him.

Picking up that thread, I remarked that in Germany his job was divided between two people: the chancellor (prime minister) and the president. One ran the government and the other welcomed the Boy Scouts, handed out awards, and represented the nation. The president nodded and named a few of the representative functions he was called upon to do that took precious time away from making the many decisions that accumulated on any given day.

To my surprise, LBJ became animated and continued with the subject. "Most evenings," he said, "I am in my pajamas, sitting up in bed at 11:00 pm. I turn on my three television sets and scan the late-night news, switching the sound between ABC, NBC, and CBS. When the news is over, I ring a bell. An assistant comes in with a big folder full of papers that I have to make decisions on. Not big decisions, mind you, but stuff requiring my consent or rejection, or needing to be passed on to a cabinet member or some other fellow to make that decision for me. Each night, I make a hundred more decisions in bed. Then I ring the bell again and the aide comes back to pick up the folder. After that, I can go to sleep, feeling that I have done the best I can for the day."

Before I could respond to this, an aide told us that the German visitor had arrived. We had to leave his peaceful vista behind and go downstairs for another political conversation.

"I am doing the best I can" was a phrase that Johnson used very often. It illustrated his feeling that he could not do complete justice to the job of president, as if anyone else could. On becoming president, he seemed to have changed into a different person. For the first time in his life, he found himself in a job that was bigger than he was. Often he seemed oppressed by the weighty responsibilities that the presidency entailed. Several times I saw him sitting silently, looking down with sadness in his eyes, his slightly bent head resting on his right hand, the index finger against his temple, the other fingers cradled under his big nose—a strange posture for a boisterous, action-oriented person.

But he was also keenly aware of the enormous powers to get things done that were now at his disposal. Getting things done had always been the hallmark of Johnson's career. However, slightly bending the truth and occasionally resorting to dirty tricks were not rejected as useful tools to get from here to there. His biographers and others have cited a number of examples. Yet it seemed to me that when he became president, he "got religion." His ethics took an almost 180 degree turn. Sure, he would still engage in arm-twisting, leaning on people, and dissimulating a little. But his moral compass was now one of honesty and trustworthiness. His word, for instance, to civil rights leaders and poor people, was as good as gold. He would try to turn his promises into reality, and he was incredibly successful in doing so.

THE VIETNAM DEBACLE

A frequent topic of discussion in Lyndon Johnson's meetings with German-speaking European leaders was the war in Vietnam. In those meetings and the accompanying classified briefings by the top political and military experts, I obtained a much clearer picture than the general public of how events fit together and how the war and the reasons for pursuing it were seen by the strategic thinkers advising the president. The government's inside view was not laid before the American public. To the public, the war was portrayed as a fight for the freedom and self-determination of South Vietnam, threatened by an invasion of the Communists in North Vietnam. To the insiders, it was a vital part of the global conflict with communism, the latest example of the "wars of national liberation" advocated by Chinese General Lin Piao.

General Lin, whose "Volunteer Army" had thwarted General MacArthur in Korea in 1952, became minister of defense of the People's Republic of China in 1959 and was later designated by the party to become Mao's successor. He lost his life in a Beijing power struggle in 1971.

His clever conquest theory was that by conducting one-by-one Communist takeovers of small nations far from the American shores, the American public would never support employing the nation's nuclear weapons to end any such conflict. In such "wars of national liberation", the Communists would support and arm the opposition, maybe even fight with them, and eventually take control of the country. In numbers of conventional soldiers, the Communist nations, led by China and the Soviet Union, would always have a vast superiority over the free world. "Going for the whole sausage" would invite a Western nuclear response. Taking one slice of the salami at a time (the "salami strategy") would not trigger such a response.

Long before Johnson, President Truman had been greatly worried about a Communist takeover in Southeast Asia. Eisenhower, who had coined the image of "falling dominoes" in 1954, saw uprisings in several countries in the region, including important ones like the Philippines and Indonesia, as indications of a larger plan for control of Southeast Asia, jeopardizing the security of the United States and friendly countries in that part of the world. LBJ had only inherited this view and the growing problem. Neither was his creation.

Many strategic thinkers in the Soviet Union, which shipped arms and supplies to North Vietnam, in China, and in the Western countries considered South Vietnam a domino in the Communist quest for world domination. It was only one front in a global war. I still believe today, as I did then, that if the global-threat view of the experts, most likely an accurate view, had been properly explained by the administration to the American public, support for the war would have been much greater. Some of the experts I listened to in those briefings contended that if, after South Vietnam, Malaysia and Indonesia would come under Communist control, the vital shipping lanes north of Australia, between the Indian Ocean and the Pacific, could have been blocked fairly easily. The free world's commerce flows through those lanes around the clock.

Cutting off that traffic would immediately have threatened the economic and military survival of countries like Japan, the Philippines, South Korea, Thailand, and even Australia and New Zealand. Certainly, the countries just mentioned shared the view of those experts, because most of them sent sizeable contingents of soldiers to fight alongside the Americans. In 1968, 50,000 South Koreans fought in Vietnam and more than 6,000 each from Thailand and Australia.

The Vietnam War took a terrible toll on President Johnson. Feeling that "he did not know a damn thing about Indochina," as he once phrased it to a visitor in my presence, and keeping in mind the terrible failure of the French in this region, he decided early on to keep his own judgment out of it and just follow the advice of his foreign policy experts, many of whom he had inherited from President Kennedy. Most of those were university professors, great theoretical minds, but somewhat short on appreciating the value of bold action on the ground. The basic reality that we had unwisely surrendered the choice of the main battlefield to the enemy, namely the swamps that suited their tactics infinitely better than ours, did not seem to influence their view of how to best conduct this war. Their overly cautious advice and constant fear of annoying other countries and further alienating American public opinion, through badly needed bold and decisive changes in the conduct of the war, allowed the enemy plenty of time to adjust. This lackluster strategic stance doomed the eventual outcome and lost the president his political power base and reputation.

But the war not only encumbered the president's other endeavors, it deeply wounded his soul. One day, I was upstairs in the living quarters of the White House with former Chancellor Ludwig Erhard. He was making a stop in Washington on his way back to Germany from South America and had been invited for a private meeting. The three of us were alone. Our conversation had gone on for forty minutes or so when it was interrupted by the loud ring of a bell. LBJ explained that it signaled a Flash on the news ticker. He left us for a moment to walk over to the machine, read the message, and tear off the printout.

He came back with a sullen expression and tears in his eyes. He told us that the message was about two dozen Marines who had been ambushed and killed by the Vietcong. The president sat back down in his chair, buried his face in his hands, and blurted out, "These are *my* boys! I sent them there. I could call them all back."

Erhard, a sensitive man, was visibly moved. He told LBJ that he was just defending Vietnam like he was defending Berlin. The entire free world was grateful for those American sacrifices. The president had trouble recovering his composure, and we took our leave. He escorted us to the elevator, operated by a Secret Service agent, and said good-bye to the chancellor. The door closed, but the elevator did not move. After ten seconds, the door opened again. The president had hurried back to us. He stretched out his hand to me and said, "Thank you so much for coming over for this. You did a great job." Then the door closed again and we moved down to the first floor. I was astonished. How could he have thought of thanking an interpreter at an anguished moment like this? I will never forget this gesture of human decency by a disconsolate president.

FORTY YEARS LATER: LOOKING BACK AT LYNDON JOHNSON

With each passing year, looking at where the American society stands today after many years of steady decline, the accomplishments of President Johnson for the betterment of our society loom larger and larger in my mind. Forever pressing forward, Americans rarely look back long enough to remember with some precision what their presidents did in office. I lectured before young Americans and Europeans in the 1980s and 1990s; most of them knew very little about LBJ that went beyond his Vietnam legacy. Obscured by the shadow of the Vietnam War, Johnson has probably become the most underrated president of the twentieth century. Conversely, Ronald Reagan, who did great damage to the American middle class and to the financial health of the nation, recently seems to have become the most overrated. Surveying LBJ's legislative accomplishments in domestic policy from today's vantage point, I am convinced that those of all other presidents of his century pale by comparison, with the only exception of Franklin Delano Roosevelt.

Capitalism and the free market economy have proven superior to all other economic systems. Even Communist China has finally learned this. But in a federation of fifty states—some strong, some weak, some vigilant, some negligent, some attuned to new realities, some very backward—the system can quickly lead to the deliberate exploitation of consumers and the environment, and to the further decline of the already disadvantaged groups in the society: the old, the poor, the racial minorities, the handicapped, and others. Only the federal government has an arm strong enough to hold back and reverse those negative trends that ultimately also work to the detriment of an economy that is largely sustained by the purchasing power of all consumers.

President Johnson was keenly aware of this and strove mightily to stem the dark side of unfettered capitalism and the discrimination against American minorities. His administration came to the aid of Native Americans with the passage of the Indian Vocational Training Act and the Indian Bill of Rights. His administration created programs to help the handicapped, with special emphasis on handicapped children. It dramatically improved the retirement and employment prospects of older Americans through the creation of Medicare and the Age Discrimination Act. It gave African Americans a bigger voice and better economic stake in the American society through the bold Civil Rights Act of 1964, the Voting Rights Act of 1965, and several programs for earlier and better education and vocational training. Totally unimaginable just a few years earlier, Johnson invited Martin Luther King, Jr. to the White House to sit down with him and plot the next moves in implementing his revolutionary and far-reaching policies. King provided the flour and the yeast. Johnson baked the bread for millions.

President Johnson made the United States a safer country. He created the Department of Transportation and gave it the tools to do its job through laws mandating highway safety, traffic safety, aircraft noise controls, and even tire safety. His administration passed laws regulating flammable fabrics, gas pipelines, wholesome poultry, and hazardous radiation. He came to the aid of young Americans through raising the minimum wage, the Juvenile Delinquency Protection Act, work programs for students, and the introduction of guaranteed student loans. He came to the aid of the poor through several antipoverty programs. He came to the aid of the environment by introducing stricter air pollution standards and by creating many new wilderness, recreation, and forest preserves. In doing the latter, he later inspired Presidents Carter and Clinton to extensively use their powers to protect large unspoiled areas of the country, not yet invaded by careless corporations.

These are only the highlights of his legislative accomplishments. The list is much longer. Remarkably, he did all this in the space of only six years. Lyndon Baines Johnson made some bad decisions about the conduct of the Vietnam War. But he made a large number of good decisions in areas of vital importance to large groups of Americans. He added a chapter to the history of the United States that Americans can point to with pride. That, above all else, is what he should be remembered for.

THE ART OF
INTERPRETATION

Few people, especially in the United States of America, have a good understanding of what a professional interpreter is and what that person does. Even journalists still confuse interpreters with translators, unaware that interpretation and translation are two different professions, requiring distinctly different methods of training and execution of the work.

With few exceptions, the description and analysis attempted here disregards what little meaningful academic literature exists on the subject in the United States. Few of those discussions are comprehensive in nature, and much of the reasoning employed is only understandable to insiders or to the theoretical linguists who have written much in this realm, filling the vacuum left by the knowledgeable professionals, who rarely put their thoughts to paper. This chapter intentionally describes the work of professional interpreters, based mostly on empirical data, and relies only to a small extent on existing theories. The description draws heavily on over thirty years of personal experience in actually doing the work, the job experience of colleagues, and recorded incidents of interpreting problems and successes.

While this analysis does not ignore the many discussions I have had on the subject while lecturing and participating in symposia at universities in the United States and Europe, the sad fact remains that few of those meetings sent me home with deeper insights or flashes of inspiration. So far, the academic dialogue has not been very productive. Many academic presentations on the subject have been self-serving in nature, aimed at scoring university points for having done research—any kind of research, meaningful or not.

This description and analysis also draws on my years of training professional interpreters. You cannot be an effective trainer without thoroughly understanding the underlying modus operandi of the successful execution of the art. That is why the most renowned training schools have seasoned professionals on their faculty. Some segments of the traditional training curriculums yield too little benefit in class and force the teacher to analyze the basics over and over again. As most of my teaching years came at the end of my career, the less productive exercises in class opened additional windows of understanding to utilizing previous interpreting experiences as more beneficial teaching tools.

So let us start with the most rudimentary definitions and gradually work our way deeper into the subject. To avoid grammatical contortions, I will use the masculine pronoun when speaking of one interpreter, with my apologies to all women interpreters.

The interpreter deals with spoken words and transfers the meaning content of those words into spoken words of another language and culture. Interpreters are always on the move, doing their work on public stages, in closed meeting rooms, in courts, in hospitals, under fire in war zones, and at the Olympic Games and other international events. They essentially work with only the knowledge in their head, because there is no time to look up things in dictionaries or in reference works. Their work product must be ready in two or three minutes (in consecutive interpretation) and in a few seconds (in simultaneous interpreting). Although interpreting in a live public environment has much in common with acting, the difference is that interpreting does not allow for prior rehearsals. It is totally immediate in nature, requiring courage and a balance of skills. The renowned Russian diplomatic interpreter Viktor Sukhodrev, when asked to describe the difference between interpreting and translating, stated that translating is like walking on a rope lying on the ground, interpreting is like walking on a rope suspended ten feet in the air.

The translator works with written documents and transfers the meaning content of written words into written words of another language. Translators do not frequently travel from site to site, like most interpreters. They usually sit in an office, in front of a computer, surrounded by a prodigious quantity of dictionaries, glossaries, encyclopedias, and other reference works. The translator may need just one minute to translate a sentence. But he may also need ten minutes or more for just one sentence if its meaning is difficult to ascertain or if that meaning is difficult to exactly replicate in the target language. He can consult his reference books or dictionaries, look things up on the Internet, get assistance from specialized computer software, or call an expert or colleague on the telephone to get help. By contrast, the interpreter is under intense time pressure. He must find an instant solution for analysis of the meaning and for the formulation in the other language. As a result, written translations done by professionals will always be more accurate than spoken translations done by professional interpreters. The translator's product is for the ages, the interpreter's for the moment.

Diff between translators & interpreters

In this description and analysis, the art of interpretation refers to the professional interpretation of spoken words. The methodology of how to do this accurately and without omissions is almost identical between any pair of languages. The profession of interpretation is usually taught at universities. It normally requires two to three years of specialized training after the student is already fluent in at least two languages. Just speaking two languages fluently is not nearly enough to make a person a good interpreter. It may allow the person to summarize the main ideas and bring across some detail, but without proper training, a complete and accurate rendition of everything the speaker said in the source language cannot be accomplished, even by people with excellent memories.

Why is professional interpretation an art and profession rather than a useful skill like driving a racecar or juggling for a circus act? Why should it need university training?

It is an art and a profession because the successful execution of complete and accurate interpretation applies the same careful methodology as is used by physicians, lawyers, engineers, and other highly skilled professionals. Let me explain.

The engineer who is supposed to build a bridge begins his work with careful analysis of many factors. If the analysis is faulty, the bridge will have serious faults. The physician begins his work with analyzing the symptoms displayed by the patient and the results of the tests he has ordered. If this analysis, called diagnosis, is incorrect, the treatment will be wrong and possibly even counterproductive. The lawyer begins each task with careful analysis of the available facts and items of evidence, depositions, and applicable laws. If this analysis is faulty, he is likely to lose his case and maybe his client.

Like all other professionals, the professional interpreter begins each phase of his work with careful analysis of many factors, of which the spoken words are but the starting point and one component. I will explain this in more detail as we move along. If his analysis is faulty, the interpreting product in the other language will be inaccurate or even counterproductive, no matter how elegantly he may phrase it. The most crucial component of all successful interpreting is a quick but careful and comprehensive analysis. Faulty analysis is the most frequent cause of error when poor interpreting occurs, in consecutive as well as in simultaneous interpretation.

Good interpreting schools teach their students how to analyze well by using a multitude of available tools and clues, just as good law schools and engineering schools do. One of those tools is good general knowledge of many fields. Where better to acquire such knowledge than at a university where a wide range of different subjects is taught in one place?

Why does a professional interpreter need to do constant analysis, and what are the most frequently encountered phenomena that require analysis?

The interpreter's work begins with hearing spoken words that are used as signals by the speaker to convey ideas, facts, or messages. This process is fraught with many dangers and pitfalls that can cause confusion.

First, the interpreter *hears* the words, he does not *see* them like the translator looking at a piece of paper. In spoken words, *colonel* and *kernel* sound exactly alike. So do *two* and *to* and *too*. So do *one* and *won* and *Juan*. There are hundreds of homonyms in any language.

Context is key !!

A much bigger obstacle to correct analysis is the multitude of meanings that are attached to the same word. Some common words carry a dozen different meanings; many words carry three or four. *multiple meaning words*

A speaker might say, "Next, I would like to speak about notes." What the interpreter needs to analyze in this sentence is the meaning of the word *notes*. Is it bank notes, musical notes, or something written down on paper? The word is just a code, a signal. The meaning currently attached to that signal is what the interpreter must quickly find.

He cannot get around this problem, because in the target language (the language of the person who listens to the interpreter), that meaning, once found, may need to be attached to an entirely different word. He cannot select a word in the target language before he has determined the exact meaning in the source language.

For instance, the English noun *stand*, depending on the meaning it is signaling, has the following equivalent nouns in German: *platz, standort, einstellung, widerstand, podium, tribüne, ständer,* and others. Although the interpreter is always pressed for time, he must wait for additional clues to determine the proper meaning before he can transfer that word or any part of a sentence into another language.

If he has to interpret a passage consisting of several sentences, it is dangerous to write down the actual words he has heard before the analysis has been completed. The three words *in the spring* can refer to a season, a source of water, or a part of a car or a clock. To make an accurate analysis of any word or group of words, the interpreter needs to track a multitude of possible clues. These include the immediate, prior, and subsequent context; his knowledge of the subject, the speaker, and the audience; the different cultural backgrounds of the speaker and the listeners; visual clues like body language or maps and charts on the wall; linguistic clues like grammar, syntax, tense, regional dialect; the rules of logic and probability; and others.

Such complicated analysis takes time, time the interpreter does not have. Training and job experience must teach him to analyze quickly and accurately. Before talking about the other difficulties constantly confronting interpreters, let me explain the three basic methods in which interpreting is done.

THE MODES OF INTERPRETATION: SENTENCE BY SENTENCE, CONSECUTIVE, AND SIMULTANEOUS

Although we are discussing professional interpretation, we should start with sentence by sentence, for that is the most common form of daily interpretation done in the United States, because—in stark contrast to most other highly developed countries—the vast majority of American interpreters are not trained professionals. As a result, the reader, in many American environments, is more likely to encounter an untrained interpreter rather than a trained professional. Encountering an untrained interpreter in Finland, France, or Germany is a rare occurrence.

A trained professional consecutive interpreter can store a passage of five to ten sentences, and even more, in his memory and notes. He can bring back all of those sentences in one piece in the other language without leaving out anything or, if he has a bad day, with a bare minimum of omissions or inaccuracies.

The amateur cannot do that and will usually beg the speaker to do just one sentence at a time. Hearing only one sentence at a time robs the interpreter of all the clues available in the next sentence or two.

Here is a simple example. One person asks the other, "Will you take your wife to London again for your vacation, like the last two summers?" This sentence contains no analytical problems for the interpreter. But now comes the answer, "Well, I have my reservations." The interpreter, if not waiting for another sentence, may assume the speaker is talking about plane and hotel reservations and puts this into the target language accordingly. But the next sentence states, "Doris complained about the London weather last year and probably would prefer Spain or Italy." The interpreter now has to backtrack and apologize, because he had to analyze without the benefit of the following sentence, he was lacking the subsequent context and, as a result, misread the meaning of *reservations*.

Professionals hate to do sentence by sentence, because it makes their analysis more difficult. But untrained interpreters are stuck with it, leading to errors and confusion for their clients. Moreover, if a speaker makes a presentation to an audience through sentence-by-sentence interpreting, it robs his speech of all flow of oratory and it robs the audience of much of their receptivity.

A curious scene, played out each day somewhere in American courtrooms, has been reported to me by many court interpreters in my interpreting classes, and has been described in discussions during meetings of interpreters or their associations.

As so many court interpreters in the United States are untrained in consecutive interpretation, their sentence-by-sentence translation often produces errors and confusion. The prosecution or the defense may challenge obvious contradictions or inaccuracies. The judge may also be confused and annoyed and finally come to the conclusion that the interpreting product is not reliable. Not knowing what makes interpreting accurate and reliable, the judge will now order the interpreter to stop translating an entire sentence in one piece: "From now on, please translate everything word for word or each part of the sentence separately."

The judge assumes that he or she and the highly educated lawyers will be in a better position to reconstruct the meaning of the sentence if only given its building blocks. Of course, this only makes the problem worse, not better. If interpreting one sentence at a time can be a mousetrap, one word or one clause at a time can be a quagmire swallowing up meaning and logical cohesion. Absent the linguistic and cultural knowledge enveloping the complex world of another language, the speaker of only his own language cannot possibly perform an accurate analysis based on the words or clauses spit out separately by the interpreter.

The logical solution to this constant courtroom dilemma is for the judges to use trained interpreters in court or to provide their interpreters, who may be very knowledgeable in legal terminology and experienced in court procedures, with reliable training in the methodology of consecutive interpretation, even if the taxpayer has to foot the bill.

Compared to the damage, the cost of training is minimal. Reliable interpreters speed up the proceedings, prevent appeals based on challenging the interpretation, keep innocents out of jail, and keep guilty defendants from going free. Moreover, at least in my opinion, not providing the defendant with a reliable interpreter is, in itself, denial of due process.

Having explored the dangers of sentence by sentence, let us return to professional interpreting. It is divided into two classic disciplines, often called "modes" in the English language: consecutive interpretation and simultaneous interpretation.

Consecutive interpretation is the most frequently used mode of professional interpretation. It is also the most reliable method. Interestingly, the few interpreters or trainers who disagree with this are almost exclusively people whose training was predominantly in simultaneous, and who have never reached a high skill level in consecutive. The reason why consecutive is more reliable is obvious. It gives the interpreter much more time for analysis and for proper formulation in the target language. Reliable interpreting stands or falls with accurate analysis.

It is called *consecutive* because the speaker will say a few sentences first while the interpreter is listening and taking his notes. Then the interpreter follows, interpreting the entire passage into the other language, without a break. When the interpreter is finished, the speaker follows with the next few sentences, and so on.

The speaker's oratory can flow, because it is not interrupted too often. The interpreter benefits because he has received a big chunk of interrelated information, enough to do a more accurate analysis and to see where the speaker is trying to lead the audience. The interpreter's rendition also will be smoother and more properly articulated, as he now knows better what to downplay and what to emphasize, just as the speaker did.

The client rightfully expects that the professional interpreter will accurately duplicate in the other language everything that was said in those few sentences, without omissions, additions, or distortions.

He also expects that the message will be delivered in the same tone of voice, retaining the points of emphasis, the humor or irony, and all relevant nuances. Obviously, this is very hard to do, even with a good speaker. It becomes a major challenge when the speaker cannot express himself well in his own language or is required—as is often the case in international conferences—to make his presentation in one of the official languages, which he may not have a good command of and may speak with an accent or improper intonation.

Given all of these requirements and intellectual challenges, how can a professional interpreter retain many sentences without losing anything?

The interpreter uses three major tools to accomplish this: anticipation, visualization, and a form of note taking that does not rely on words and duplicates the structure of the message, displaying it like a photograph. Professional interpreters do not write words down horizontally, as they were taught in most languages in school. Instead, they write down the meaning and structure of the passage vertically, using a narrow pad, usually only four to five inches in width. Only a few words appear in their notes, and those are usually abbreviated.

We will discuss professional notation in more detail a little later. Let us deal with anticipation and visualization first.

The interpreter knows that most of the sentences that he will have to interpret have the same basic structure. He knows that human intercourse is essentially two-dimensional.

Who is doing what to whom? What is doing what to what? What is doing what to whom? He also knows that most sentences are carried by an action verb and a lesser number by the interchangeable descriptive verbs *to be* or *to have*, e.g., "The sky *is* blue" or "The sky *has* a blue color." He expects an agent and a recipient of the action in each action sentence. He already anticipates this and has the structure laid out in his mind before the speaker has begun his sentence.

He further anticipates that the upcoming action verb, let us say "to build," is most likely going to be qualified in one or more of the following ways: *when* it was built, *where* it was built, *how* it was built, or *why* it was built. In his mind, he always has an anticipative antenna out that asks, "Did he say when? Did he say where?", and so on.

I call this type of listening to spoken words "strategic listening." Schools and universities spend years teaching us strategies for effective speaking and writing. You rarely hear of a course in effective listening. As all successful politicians, detectives, and journalists know, it all begins with effective listening. Interpreters, too, need a logically structured and anticipative approach when listening to spoken words.

This orderly anticipation allows the professional interpreter to quickly sort the stream of words pouring into his ears into a meaningful structure. This structure is also duplicated in his memory, his notes, and his visualization.

Now let us discuss how the interpreter uses his memory.

The three major tools of holding information accurately in the interpreter's short-term memory are *visualization, association,* and *anticipation.*

The neurons in the brain respond to various stimuli: sound, sight, touch, smell, and taste. If an event is recorded via more than one of those stimuli, the brain can analyze and remember it better. If a fire were to break out in the hotel where you are staying, for example, you may see and hear it and also smell the smoke. Having the event recorded through three different channels, the brain will instantly and accurately identify it and remember it better.

As far as seeing the event, curiously, it seems to make no difference to the activation of the neurons in the brain whether it is seen with the physical eyes or whether it is seen with the inner eye via imagining the event, like during a dream. As soon as the interpreter has heard the words and analyzed their meaning, he will now visualize the result of this analysis with his inner eye. If he hears that a tornado has destroyed a hospital in Oklahoma City, he will visualize a tornado, a devastated hospital, and Oklahoma City. He may never have been to Oklahoma City and not know what it looks like. That does not matter. As long as he imagines any cityscape to which he now assigns the value of Oklahoma City, the neurons in his brain have been activated twice, through the analysis of the sound and through the inner image. If the interpreter does not know that a nuclear particle accelerator has a doughnut shape, he may as well visualize it in the shape of a kitchen refrigerator with a nuclear warning sign on it. His neurons have now created that image and assigned the technical label to it. When that image flashes up in his mind later, he will remember *nuclear particle accelerator.*

In trying to remember the event when he has to describe it in the other language three minutes later, the interpreter, in addition to consulting his notes, now has two shelves in his short-term memory to go to for help: the sound analysis shelf and the visualization shelf, with one complementing or substituting for the other. One reason why most people remember the experience of making love so vividly rests on the fact of having recorded the event in their brain via so many different stimuli: having touched, seen, heard, and smelled the other person.

There is good reason why perfumes are such big business. They add another dimension. By continuously using two of his senses—sound and sight—the interpreter can remember better.

It has been known for centuries that _association_ aids recall. The trick here consists of assigning something just heard to a similar item already stored and frequently called up in your memory. Let us assume we need to remember a particular number, say, 4, 15, 18, or 31. Every year we are reminded that July 4 is Independence Day, that the tax return is due on April 15, that Mother's birthday is on September 18, and that Halloween is on October 31. Each year, the memory reactivates its storage shelves for those events.

The interpreter uses these existing shelves for recalling the numbers, as soon as he hears them, through association with those events. He can also use the image of Independence Day when he has to remember the month of July.

Finally, _anticipation,_ an important tool in strategic listening, is also a helpful memory aid. Professional interpreters constantly try to anticipate what the speaker is likely to say next. First, this activity helps the interpreter to stay alert and interested, because he is playing a little guessing game, not too different from bridge or poker. This side activity also reduces the stress that constantly accompanies interpreting work.

But anticipation also helps the interpreter's memory, similar to association. Example: one diplomat says to the other, "Next month, we'll see each other again at the European Regional Conference in …" The interpreter knows that those meetings usually alternate between Brussels, Paris, and Rome. Last year's meeting was in Rome. He anticipates hearing "Paris." This activates neurons in his brain, storing his act of anticipation and expecting the validation through the spoken word "Paris." But the word he hears is "Brussels." He anticipated wrong. Whether the anticipation is right or wrong, having created a special little brain shelf awaiting the validation or negation of "Paris" helps the interpreter to remember "Brussels" better. His brain was ready to put a city on that shelf.

PROFESSIONAL INTERPRETING NOTES

Apart from effective listening techniques and skillful use of the memory, an interpreter has little chance to advance to the senior journeyman or the master level in consecutive interpretation without having learned to take the type of notes that are most useful for a complete and accurate rendition of any passage consisting of three sentences or more.

The conventional way of writing down the sequence of the words, either horizontally or vertically or in shorthand, is useless and counterproductive.

First of all, the interpreter does not have the time to do that. Conventional writing is so slow and consumes so much of the brain's energy and neuron flow that the interpreter has neither the time nor the energy left for proper strategic listening and meaning analysis or for efficient use of his memory. So, why take any notes at all? Without the assistance of notes, many difficult interpreting tasks cannot be performed properly, even by people of great intelligence and with exceptional memories.

Second, the essence of good interpretation is the correct analysis of the meaning behind the words. Those words have to be analyzed while they are being heard. The notes should reflect the product and structure of that analysis. If the interpreter spends his time writing down all or most of the words, he cannot productively analyze while the speaker is speaking; he misses most of his body language, tone, emphasis, irony, and so on. Nor can he manipulate his memory properly, because his energy and concentration is flowing onto the paper. He is now forced to analyze a written text like a translator. Translators have time to do that. Interpreters do not.

Third, the notes are needed to assist the memory in replicating the structure and sequence of the thoughts expressed by the speaker. Thus the notation must reflect the same structure that underlies the process of strategic listening. *Who does what to whom? When? Where? Why? How?* The analytical thinking process of the interpreter must be reflected in the structure of his notes, so that the two can complement and assist each other.

Let us take a 130-word passage from a business meeting and see how this passage is replicated in interpreting notes. This is a straightforward, fact-oriented statement, requiring little analysis.

Mr. Chairman, Members of the Board,

Three months ago, you gave me the task of providing you with a first estimate of the cost for the planned new headquarters building. The figures that I am putting before you today should be seen with a margin of error of plus or minus 15 percent.

There are four major cost categories to be considered: the acquisition of the land, the architectural design, the construction cost, and moving the headquarters thirty miles to the Ronald Reagan Industrial Complex.

Let me begin with the purchase of the land. We would need to acquire 16.5 acres. The current price per acre is $76,000, for a total cost of about $1.25 million.

However, a curtailed lot of fourteen acres, with less landscaping, would save $190,000.

The illustration shows you what a journeyman interpreter's notes on this passage may look like. A master-level consecutive interpreter would get along with even fewer notes.

The interpreter leaves an imaginary small margin on the left. Into that margin go addresses, like "Mr. Chairman," indications of change of speaker, and most importantly, all conjunctions that change the direction of the train of thought. Examples for such conjunctions would be *however, yet, but, although, nevertheless,* and so on.

For the interpreter, these are very much interchangeable. In the illustration, the interpreter has substituted *but if* for *however,* because it is shorter and a clearer signal for the expressed thought.

Into the space next to the imagined margin goes the subject or the *agent* in an action sentence. If there are several subjects, they are lined up vertically, not horizontally. Thus, that vertical column is reserved for subjects, making it easy to quickly locate them on each page.

Next to the subject, one column over and one line down from the subject comes the verb, which usually denotes an action (except in descriptive sentences). Here again, this vertical space is reserved for the verbs that are the backbone of the sentence. The interpreter can quickly find the all-important action verb later, because he knows exactly where to look for it. The structure of the page duplicates the pattern of *Who is doing what to whom? What is doing what to what?,* resembling the typical discourse and his approach to listening.

Everything else is found on the right half of the narrow page. All recipients of the action, or in grammatical terms, objects, are lined up vertically, too, like subjects and verbs.

The notation example in the illustration shows the many ways in which the interpreter tries to keep his notes to a minimum of wrist strokes to conserve time and energy for the important tasks of strategic listening and analysis of the meaning behind the words. Long words are abbreviated or shorter synonyms (words with the same meaning) are substituted. The interpreter writes *buy* instead of *acquire* or *purchase*. For *however*, he could also have used the much shorter synonym *yet*, which has the same meaning.

If no short synonym quickly comes to mind, words are abbreviated. *HQB* for *headquarters building*, *c'd* for *could*, *s'd* for *should*, *ld* for *land*, *arch* for *architectural design*.

To avoid words altogether, each professional consecutive interpreter has, over time, assembled a collection of ideograms, also called interpreting symbols. Such an ideogram represents an idea or a concept and is used in place of nouns, verbs, adjectives, or adverbs, reflecting that concept or idea. In our example, the concept *estimate* is represented by a horizontal line with bubbles rising from it. For the interpreter, the bubbles stand for the basic concept of *guess, estimate, assume,* and so on. In the sentence at hand, it represents the idea behind the noun *estimate*.

Let us look at the notation for *Ronald Reagan Industrial Complex*. Here the interpreter has used a combination of abbreviation and ideograms. He has abbreviated *Ronald Reagan* as *RR*. But *RRIC* is not a standard abbreviation, and there is a slight risk that it may not trigger the correct image in his mind. For *Industrial*, he uses his ideogram for *industry*, which is a little smokestack; for *Complex*, he uses his ideogram for *complicated, tricky, convoluted, complex*, which is a simple representation of a knot. Having the ideograms on paper ensures that he will not misinterpret a four-letter abbreviation.

The words *today* and *seen* are also written in ideograms in our illustration. Professional interpreters know their ideograms so well that they automatically flow onto the paper as soon as the corresponding concept has been distilled from the words.

How many ideograms are in a typical collection? I have worked with hundreds of professional colleagues over my long interpreting career and have asked quite a few of them how many ideograms they have. The answers have varied from 50 to 300, with master-level interpreters usually having a smaller number than colleagues at somewhat lower skill levels. My own stable of ideograms has varied over the years from between 90 and 130. If you invent an ideogram, but find that you do not use it enough or misread it occasionally, it is better to quickly drop it from the collection. On the other hand, if a colleague has invented a brilliant symbol, you ask him if you can use it and quickly add it to your own repertoire.

Interpreting ideograms are related to pictograms that are used in some languages, like Chinese, in place of the individual letters of European languages. In Chinese, to record the word for *tree,* you draw a simple representation of a tree. By drawing three tree symbols, you have written down *forest.* Interpreters who have mother tongues that use pictograms have a much easier time building a collection of ideograms and will usually use more of them, even if their notation language is a European language. We will discuss the concept of notation language a little later.

When, as a teacher, I had my interpreting students in class design ideograms, students from Japan or China quickly came up with usable ideograms a little more often than students from language cultures that do not use pictograms. One Japanese student suggested a triangle with the apex at the top for the concept of *woman* (representing a skirt), then put a little circle inside the triangle for the concept of *pregnancy*. The class loved it, and most students adopted those ideograms.

One major advantage of employing ideograms in notation is that they immediately cancel out the actual words used in the source language to describe that concept. Not having the words used by the speaker on paper eliminates the danger of trying to use the same words in the target language, especially when the interpreter is tired at the end of a long day. For instance, if the statement, "Yesterday, there was a demonstration in front of the White House," has to be translated into French, a tired interpreter looking at the word *demonstration* might just use it in French, because the identical word exists in that language. However, the correct translation is *manifestation*. Working from an ideogram, an interpreter who is fluent in French would never make that mistake.

Even interpreters who use a lot of ideograms cannot avoid using many words in their notes. As we saw earlier, those words are often abbreviated or replaced by a shorter synonym. Being forced to record words on paper brings up an interesting problem. What language should an interpreter use as his notation language? Should it be the language he hears (i.e., the source language) or the language he has to translate into (i.e., the target language)? When an interpreter works alone, the source and target languages constantly alternate. First he has to translate into English, then into Japanese. If he picks the source language, he has to take notes in two languages. If he picks the target language, he also has to take notes in two languages.

Taking notes in two or more languages is not a good idea. Interpreters are always under pressure. They have to listen carefully, analyze, memorize, take notes, and find the correct formulations in the target language. They cannot stare at a hastily written word on their notepad and not be sure what language they are looking at. There are hundreds of thousands of words in each language. They should always take their notes in the same language regardless of whether it is the source or the target language.

Now, if an interpreter decides he will always take notes in the same language, that decision brings up the next problem. Which language should he use? He may be fluent in three languages. Is it not safest to stick with his mother tongue?

The most frequently used language combination for interpreting work in the United States is English-Spanish. Most of the interpreters working in this combination have Spanish as their mother tongue. Naturally, they will be inclined to use Spanish as their notation language.

However, seasoned professionals will usually select English. Why? The main reason is that English allows you to save time and wrist strokes. Many of the most often occurring verbs in the English language have only one syllable, while in Spanish they often have two or three. Let us name a few: to live and to die, to love and to hate, to come and to go, to push and to pull, to walk and to run, to buy and to sell, to rise and to fall, to wake and to sleep, to drive and to fly. The auxiliary verbs usually are monosyllabic: to get, let, make, put. The same is true of many key nouns and adjectives.

The words written down in the notation language have little value to the interpreter beyond being indicators of the analyzed meaning, similar to ideograms. The interpreter will hear *enfants* and write down *kids,* because it is shorter than *children.* But when interpreting into English, he will say "children." *Kids* was just an indicator of the meaning, of the semantic content of *enfants*. If the speaker says *fledgling company,* the interpreter will write down *startup*, a shorter synonym reflecting the same idea.

Most of my interpreting was between English and German. German words can be even longer than Spanish words. Therefore, I selected English as my notation language, even though German is my mother tongue. Early in my career, before my French became rusty, I would occasionally work informal meetings from French into German. I was listening to French, taking my notes in English, and speaking in German. In those meetings, my notation language was neither the source nor the target language. It did not matter. The language that saves the most time and most wrist strokes is usually the most efficient notation language. Notes: Meaning > Word

Let us now proceed to explain the other mode of professional interpretation.

Simultaneous interpretation is just as old as consecutive interpretation, although books and articles on the subject often assert that it came into existence with the founding of the League of Nations after Word War I, or later during the Nuremberg Trials after World War II. The assumption here is that simultaneous interpretation is tied to the use of electrical or electronic equipment.

But even with electrical equipment, primitive at it was at the time, there already were a few experiments in simultaneous interpreting at conferences in Germany and Russia before the League of Nations was founded. Long before Edison ushered in the electric age and laid the foundation for electronics with his invention of the vacuum tube, simultaneous interpreting (without equipment) had existed for centuries. It was done through whispering the translation into the ears of the listeners. This technique is still used today, for instance, when a diplomatic interpreter at a press conference whispers into the ear of one leader what another leader is saying to the press in another language.

There were other reasons why simultaneous interpreting was occasionally preferred, even in ancient history. If a conqueror like Alexander, Caesar, or Genghis Khan had a captive king or general standing in front of him for interrogation or negotiation, he often did not want other leaders or generals in attendance to hear the translated information. Knowledge is power. He would instruct the interpreter to whisper the translation simultaneously into his ear only. Later he would parcel out to the others only what he wanted them to know, keeping some precious information all to himself. There is little historical information about the lifespan of those interpreters.

While in consecutive interpretation the interpreter waits until the speaker gives him a chance to interpret a few sentences or maybe one long sentence, here the interpreter does not wait but speaks simultaneously in the target language while the speaker is moving along in the source language. The simultaneity is not total, because the interpreter must have understood the meaning hidden behind a few words before he can transfer this into the other language. He will be a few words, half a sentence, or an entire sentence behind the speaker, but he does not pause. The time gap between the speaker and the interpreter is known as *décalage* in the profession, a French word describing the gap between two successive actions.

If the information in the source language is readily understandable, for instance, "on the fourteenth of July, in Paris," the interpreter will instantly put it into the other language, but if he cannot yet comprehend what is meant by a few words, he will have to wait for some subsequent context before he can continue in the target language.

As we discussed earlier, the most important clue to the meaning of a sentence is often the action verb: *spend* or *save, agree* or *disagree, increase* or *decrease.* In some languages, like German and Mongolian, the action verb often comes at the very end of the sentence, forcing interpreters to fall an entire sentence behind before they can start the English, French, or Italian sentence, where the grammar usually calls for the action verb out front. That is why there are more simultaneous interpreters offering their services from English into German than from German into English. The German syntax makes one combination much more stressful than the other, but the pay is the same.

Simultaneous interpretation confronts the interpreter with two considerable obstacles to the task of correct meaning analysis: lack of analysis time and lack of subsequent context. We discussed lack of subsequent context (clues available from the next sentence or more) in the earlier description of sentence-by-sentence interpretation. The lack of time for analysis is an even bigger problem in simultaneous interpreting and the most frequent source of meaning errors and poor phrasing in the target language. This problem gets compounded further if the interpreters must deal with subjects that they are not familiar with or were not previously briefed on, or if they have to deal with poor speakers, foreign accents, conflicting grammatical structures, or audio problems caused by bad equipment or inattentive technicians manning the switches.

Before we look deeper into the pernicious time problem, let us discuss why and where the much more costly mode of simultaneous interpretation is used in the first place. Most of us have seen it employed at the United

Nations or the European Union. These are the two largest employers of simultaneous interpreters in the world.

Consecutive interpretation has many advantages. It is cheaper, is more accurate, and uses no complicated equipment (only pen and paper are needed). However, because the speaker and the interpreter speak one after the other, it requires twice as much time. This is usually an acceptable trade-off for considerable cost savings and greater accuracy of the translation as long as only two languages are involved. With three languages, part of the audience will have to sit through two language versions they cannot understand before the information finally reaches them in their own language. That should only be done when there is no other choice. When four or more languages are involved, simultaneous interpretation becomes mandatory.

Sessions of the United Nations, the European Union, and a few other international organizations employ a large number of official languages, forcing the use of an elaborate and costly setup for reliable simultaneous interpretation from and into each language.

The method is also used every day in hundreds of meetings around the world when scientists, business leaders, educators, lawyers, politicians, and others discuss transnational issues or the specialties of their field.

Apart from the necessity to use simultaneous interpretation when several languages are involved, in the last three decades or so, it has been increasingly employed to effect timesavings, even when only two languages are present.

A good example is American courts. The judges' dockets and our jails are more crowded than ever before. Defendants and witnesses who cannot speak English are more numerous than ever before. Furnishing an interpreter to defendants who cannot understand or speak English sufficiently is now mandatory. While consecutive interpretation was standard in judicial proceedings as late as the 1950s and 1960s, employing simultaneous interpretation to save time has since grown exponentially in the courts. This is regrettable and counterproductive for a number of reasons, especially if only one interpreter is used. Those reasons will become clear to the reader from what is discussed later in this chapter.

At this point, an explanation of the logistics of simultaneous interpretation is needed for the reader who is not familiar with it. Otherwise, some subsequent points will be difficult to understand.

For the listener, even more so than for the interpreter, the annoying problem accompanying this mode of interpretation is that there are two languages entering the ear at the same time: the source language and the target language. In consecutive interpretation, one follows the other, eliminating this inconvenience and barrier to focused concentration. To minimize the distraction of having to listen to two languages, whispering is used in the target language for one or two listeners or speaking in a low voice, for which the profession uses an Italian term *sotto voce*, for a small group of listeners. However, for a large group, sound separation is necessary, both for the interpreters and for the listeners.

If a conference with several languages needs simultaneous interpretation, the conference needs to either pick a site where permanent interpreting booths are already present or install booths for the duration of the meetings. The purpose of the booths is total sound separation. Each booth normally contains two interpreters, who take turns doing this strenuous work. They listen through earphones to the various speakers and speak their interpretation into a microphone. The conference participants also have earphones and a dial with which they can choose the language they want to listen to. There may be an English booth, a French booth, a Russian booth, and so on. By dialing a particular booth, participants can hear the translation in that language.

For the interpreters, simultaneous interpretation is much more stressful and tiring than consecutive. Imagine driving down a major highway in the center lane, with a lot of traffic in all three lanes going in the same direction. Suddenly, a car from the other side of the road, going in the opposite direction, crosses over the grassy median and comes toward you while you are doing sixty-five miles per hour. A shot of adrenalin zips through your body and your brain. You now need to make many observations and decisions in split seconds. What cars are in the lanes to your left and right, and how far apart are they? Can you squeeze over to one lane or the other by rapidly accelerating, or do you need to hit the brakes? Is the wayward car likely to hit a car in the left lane first and push that car into you? The car behind you shows up very close in your rear mirror. Is it not better to brake hard and be rear-ended by it than to be hit from the front? Or is it too late for that option?

This is only a slightly exaggerated description of what accurate simultaneous interpretation is all about. You cannot do it at a normal level of adrenalin. You have to make innumerable decisions in seconds and split seconds. Like that six-lane road, your brain often has to go in two opposite directions at the same time, while monitoring traffic in all six lanes.

Let me be more specific. An interpreter sits in the booth, translating from German to English. While he is listening to a German sentence, part of his brain is busy finding the right English formulations for the previously heard German sentence that he has already begun to speak into the microphone in English. The semantic content of that sentence is stored in his memory. He needs to track it to make sure there are no omissions. Another part of his memory is meanwhile busy storing the new sentence that is coming into his ears. Another part of his brain is monitoring what he is currently saying in English into the microphone to make sure it is grammatically correct, is phrased so that this particular audience can properly understand it, and corresponds in substance to the information being tracked by one part of his memory. Suddenly, he has trouble analyzing the meaning of the new sentence before he has heard the key verb. That verb in German is not coming until the very end of that sentence, forcing him to memorize everything he has heard before the verb, even though it does not make any sense to him as yet.

Finally, he understands. He must now reel that sentence out of his memory from one direction while he is putting it into English in the other grammatical direction. But while he is doing that, a new German sentence has begun and must be analyzed simultaneously. That analysis, apart from linguistic and immediate contextual clues, includes making sure that what he is hearing is logical and that it corresponds to what he knows about the subject from a preconference briefing and to what he has heard from the speaker earlier in the conference. In the middle of that sentence, the conference chair, who is one of the persons listening to the interpreter's English, has briefly taken off his headset to greet a dignitary who has approached him.

The interpreter in the booth needs to notice such things. That is why the booth has glass in the front through which speakers, graphics on the wall, and the room can be visually monitored. The conference chair is the most important client of the interpreter. The interpreter, who normally is too busy to write anything down, starts to make some notes, so he can later give the chair a summary of the three or four sentences he is now missing out on. When the chairman has his earphones back on, the interpreter gives him the quick summary. This puts him two and a half sentences behind the speaker. He now has to speed up all of his analysis and speaking actions, because his brain cannot keep on memorizing two and a half sentences. He quickly needs to get back within one sentence. Of course, he could just drop two sentences. Remember Rosemary Woods and the missing eighteen seconds? He may never hear the end of it. Nobody ever got punished for criticizing an interpreter.

I hope the reader is beginning to understand that accurate simultaneous interpretation is fiendishly difficult and very tiring. Interpreters normally get rotated every thirty minutes, because the brain cannot reliably sustain this many actions any longer than that. The interpreters at the European Union once went on strike, contending that thirty minutes was too much. They demanded a twenty-minute rotation.

If interpreters are forced to continue longer than half an hour without a break, their performance will deteriorate gradually and rather rapidly. Many judges in American courts work with only one simultaneous interpreter for hours. If they believe that they are getting an accurate translation, they are sadly mistaken. Even master-level interpreters start having trouble after thirty minutes. But they are experienced enough to minimize the damage by leaving out redundancies and resorting to occasional summaries that leave out nothing of importance. But very few masters of the art ever work in American courts. They are paid twice as much (and more) in other environments.

As good interpretation stands or falls with correct analysis of the message contained in the spoken words, having only seconds available for that analysis, rather than minutes in consecutive, makes complete and accurate simultaneous interpretation an extremely stressful exercise.

In my long interpreting career, I have seen interpreters mangle the headset cords with their fidgeting hands until they broke. I have seen women interpreters unbutton their dresses in the booth until they fell open, never knowing what they were doing, because of the intense concentration on their work. I have seen interpreters, the late Margareta Bowen of Georgetown University comes to mind, go into the booth with a ball of putty or wax to constantly knead in order to ease the nervous pressures.

It is true that master-level simultaneous interpreters are usually well paid. But they earn every dollar the hard way, abusing their minds and jeopardizing their nervous systems (and occasionally their very sanity).

While I was a staff interpreter at the Department of State in Washington, I once was stuck with having to do simultaneous interpreting by myself all day at a highly classified military meeting. Nobody else was available that day who also held the three needed clearances: Top Secret, NATO COSMIC, and Q (the Q clearance has to do with nuclear weapons).

I had to work in the booth in both directions, into English and into German. This also necessitated flipping a switch in the booth each time I changed languages. Apart from a brief lunch, there was one ten-minute break in the morning and one in the afternoon. That meant interpreting four stretches of almost two hours each without a break, handling highly complex and technical subjects into two target languages.

When it was over, I stepped out of the booth and leaned against a wall. My heart was still racing from all the adrenalin. My hands were trembling as I fingered my pockets for a cigarette (at that time, I was still stupid enough to smoke). My brain, finally released from all the torture, went into total limbo. My eyes were closed when I heard a voice calling out, "Harry, Harry." I opened my eyes to blankly stare at the man standing in front of me. I did not recognize or acknowledge him. "Harry, do you hear me?" he kept asking. "It's me, Bill." At last, my brain was able to recognize who was in front of me. It was William Krimer, the senior Russian staff interpreter and a good friend, who had come down to the conference room to see if my ordeal was over. Bill was not annoyed that I did not recognize him. He was a fellow professional who well understood why I was in that condition. Simultaneous interpreting can so exhaust your brain that you can no longer recognize a close friend who is standing in front of you or recognize his voice.

RELAY INTERPRETING

The official languages of the European Union have recently grown beyond twenty. The annual cost of interpreting and translating that many languages is about to break the one billion dollar mark. It would be much higher if relay interpreting were not used.

Let us look at a hypothetical meeting in which nine languages are allowed for simultaneous interpretation. The number of directions (English to French, French to Italian, Italian to English, etc.) would be 72 ($9 \times 9 - 9$). The Italian booth would need to have sixteen interpreters assigned, if each could only translate from one other language into

Italian, considering that simultaneous interpreters need to be rotated every half hour.

To reduce the number of needed interpreters, two methods are used at the European Union, the United Nations, and several other international organizations. The first is the requirement that interpreters must be able to translate from two acquired languages into their mother tongue. In other words, they must be fluent in three languages.

The second is the use of relay interpreting. Let us assume an interpreter in the Italian booth needs to interpret a German speaker into Italian but does not understand German. However, the interpreter is fluent in Spanish. The interpreter can now switch his headset from listening to the German speaker to listening to the Spanish booth, in which another interpreter is putting the German into Spanish. This method has its faults, but they are unavoidable when so may directions need to be served. The client now listening to the Italian booth is, so to speak, buying a fake Gucci bag. He does not get the translation from the original but a translation of a translation. Every mistake made by the first interpreter is automatically repeated by the second interpreter, who also may add his own mistakes from errors in analysis. Things can get really treacherous if a third interpreter now tries to relay from the Italian booth, a translation of a translation from a translation.

The relay is less problematic when all interpreters are fluent in the same language, today usually English, a few decades ago usually French. If only five languages are involved, that is twenty directions, but if all interpreters can understand English well, the chief interpreter can put the best and most experienced interpreters into the English booth. These interpreters will make very few mistakes that would be repeated down the line.

When I was assigned to doing English relay, I always stayed away from fancy terms and formulations. I would stick to the most simple and direct expressions to make the analysis easier for the interpreter relaying from me, who could not hear the original. Because this deviation from an interpreter's usual handling of the target language puts an additional burden on the brain, plus the constant awareness that any mistake made will be duplicated by others down the line, getting assigned to the relay booth is not warmly welcomed by some simultaneous interpreters.

PRESIDENTIAL VIGNETTES

RICHARD M. NIXON

1969–1974

A QUANTUM LEAP FROM RESPECT TO DISTRUST

Lyndon Johnson did not tolerate a shoddy performance by any professional. He would rudely scold interpreters or the technicians operating the interpreting equipment if they fell down on the job. But he had great respect for professional interpreters. He understood the difficulties and complexities of the art and admired its top practitioners. He frequently thanked or praised interpreters privately and even in public.

This cooperative attitude, particularly toward the professional diplomatic interpreters sent routinely to the White House from the Department of State, vanished with the advent of the Nixon administration.

In 1963, I had become a naturalized American citizen. Like many of us, I virtually never failed to vote, in big elections and in small ones. In 1968, I had voted against Nixon. I knew precious little about him, but I knew that he had worked with Senator Joseph McCarthy. I thought McCarthy to be one of the most despicable and untrustworthy American politicians I had ever read about, with no respect for the American Constitution. As Nixon had collaborated with him, I inferred that he, too, could not be trusted. That may have been the only reason why I voted against him. My vote did not keep him from winning, and he became the second president I now had to interpret for.

So I was curious what the real Nixon would be like. Shortly after he took office, I was sitting in the cabinet room of the White House with a sizeable German delegation, headed by Chancellor Willy Brandt, and with a few of Nixon's cabinet members, waiting for the president to arrive. He was a few minutes late.

When he entered, I had my eyes fixed on him. It created a first impression that would never leave me. He sort of slinked into the room, a couple of briefing books under his arm, looking around with suspicious and cold eyes, his head slightly bowed, and hurried toward his seat in the middle of the table. A voice inside me said, "My God, he looks like an accountant coming in to face a board of inquiry into an embezzlement. What a contrast to Lyndon Johnson!" His first entrance contributed nothing to improve my opinion of him.

President Nixon asks German Chancellor Kiesinger
to accompany him into the Oval Office. Obst is
waiting in the background. *White House photo*

For a professional interpreter, liking or disliking an important client
creates emotional hurdles that you need to jump over every day. You
have sworn an oath of loyalty to your government, and professional
ethics forbids you from being anything but totally impartial. That is
often not easy to do. As an interpreter, you have an arsenal of options to
make the leaders you like sound better and the leaders you dislike sound
worse. And there is sometimes a little mischievous elf jumping around
in your brain that says, "Sock it to him. He deserves it." Or it may

whisper, "What a stupid remark from your favorite president. Help him out. Make him sound better." Being impartial is easy when the client has no personal place in your heart. But when you really like or dislike somebody, you are in for a battle with your conscience many a day.

As I found out later, suspicion and distrust were the hallmark of this president and his inner circle. This attitude extended to the professional interpreters serving the White House. Most of us came from Language Services at the Department of State, an office that had loyally served the president and vice president since its creation by Thomas Jefferson in 1790. No leak of secrets or disloyal act has ever been traced to a staff interpreter from the department, at least not in the last hundred years or so where we have a record to look at. But Nixon's White House looked upon us with great suspicion.

Every time I would enter the Oval Office to interpret, I would say, "Good morning, Mr. President!" or "Good afternoon, Mr. President!" I do not recall ever getting a response from Nixon. All other presidents would return the greeting or at least give me a nod or a friendly smile. Nixon kept a cold distance, and some of my colleagues told me they now felt looked upon as if they were walking dictating machines. When Nixon traveled overseas, he usually preferred to rely on the foreign interpreters or take somebody, not from State, who was trusted. Although I interpreted for him many times in Washington, I traveled abroad with him only once, to Austria in June of 1974. As we were now largely out in the cold, trusted friends of the White House or foreign interpreters would often take our place.

VERNON A. WALTERS

A good example of a trusted interpreter was Vernon A. Walters, originally a military intelligence officer in World War II. Walters was fluent in French and later picked up a good command of Portuguese, which he was able to widen while stationed in Brazil, and also a reasonable command of Italian while stationed in Rome. He also had studied some German, Spanish, and Russian, but never reached the depth of comprehension and expression in those languages that are required of a professional diplomatic interpreter. I know this from my own observations and from the observations of my professional colleagues. Walters was highly intelligent and always had the ability to absorb foreign languages rapidly.

In the Second World War, he sort of stumbled into interpreting because the U.S. Armed Forces never seem to have reliable interpreters while in the field. Initially, his language skills were used for the interrogation of prisoners in Africa and elsewhere. Before long, he was interpreting for generals like Mark Clark, George Marshall, and later, Eisenhower. Assignments as military attaché followed in Brazil, Italy, and France, and he quickly climbed the military ladder to three-star general; he was even appointed deputy director of the Central Intelligence Agency by President Nixon in May 1972.

When Eisenhower became president, General Walters became a presidential interpreter and was often used by Nixon in that capacity, even though he was now a general and occasionally interpreted in his general's uniform, drawing salutes from lower ranks while he was interpreting airport speeches or other remarks in public. But he never had had any professional interpreter training and did not know how to take interpreting notes with vertical notation and ideograms. He learned from bitter experience that longhand notations were counterproductive. Thus he resolved to always interpret from memory only, even passages of five minutes or longer.

When Nixon went to Europe in February 1969, Walters, then attaché in Paris, traveled with him from Washington on *Air Force One* and interpreted in Belgium. The next stop was Bonn, where Chancellor Kurt Georg Kiesinger gave a lunch for Nixon in the absence of his German interpreter. Kiesinger launched into a long toast and Walters volunteered to interpret from German and did a creditable job. He then proceeded to interpret for President Giuseppe Saragat and Pope Paul VI in Rome in Italian. The next stop was easy for him: Paris and President De Gaulle. In October 1971, Walters even did some interpreting in Spanish in Madrid during a talk between Nixon and Admiral Carrero Blanco.

My first encounter with Walters was at the end of March 1969 during a White House reception given by the recently inaugurated Nixon for foreign leaders attending the funeral of President Eisenhower. Toward the end of the East Room reception, Nixon was seeing some of the leaders individually in the upstairs living quarters. I was there to cover the chancellors of Austria and Germany as well as the Swiss president. When Chancellor Klaus of Austria, with whom I had just finished a conversation with Prime Minister Trudeau of Canada, was asked upstairs, I was surprised to find Vernon Walters, on crutches because of a skiing accident, hovering by the door. As Klaus was entering the door, Walters was maneuvering to get between him and me to do the interpreting in German. I was not on crutches, so I got a step ahead of him, slipped through the door, and said to him, as I was closing it, "I can handle this." Fortunately, he did not protest, then or later. The meeting was brief and friendly and easy to interpret.

Three or four years later, I found myself in another meeting with Walters at Camp David in the Catoctin Mountains of Maryland. It was a highly classified military briefing for German Defense Minister Leber, given by Secretary of Defense James Schlesinger. The logistical setup at Aspen Lodge was an interpreter's nightmare. I was seated six chairs away from the secretary, who was mumbling and smoking a pipe. To his left sat Vernon Walters, at that time deputy director of the CIA. Three or four times I had to ask Schlesinger to repeat sentences containing important information; I simply could not understand him because of the bad acoustics and his mumbling.

Schlesinger and the general in charge of the meeting, not Walters, were visibly displeased by this. During the morning coffee break, the general hauled me into a side room and gave me a royal dressing-down, but refused to reseat me after I had explained my hearing problem. "You do not interrupt the secretary of defense!" he shouted at me. I told him that I would not translate important information that I was not sure of and would have to ask the secretary to repeat again, if necessary. He ordered me not to do it and just translate as best I could. I refused. He grew red in the face, drew a step nearer to me, and bellowed, "Young man [I was already over forty], do you realize that you are speaking to a three-star general?"

Now, I come from a long line of Prussians. Prussians, like Texans, do not readily quake in their boots when shouted at. Surprised that he was trying to pull rank on a civilian, I looked him straight in the eyes and said in a firm voice, "General, do you realize that you may be speaking to a five-star interpreter?" For a moment, I thought he would kill me. But suddenly, he broke out laughing and said, "This is the biggest piece of chutzpah I have ever heard in my life. I'll reseat you." I did not quite get the seat I wanted, but most of my problem was solved.

Later during the meeting, I had to interpret the term "surveillance," for which I said in German "*Überwachung*," as it made sense in the context. During the next break, Vernon Walters pulled me aside and said, "The German term for surveillance is *Horchposten*, not *Überwachung*." I thanked him politely for the correction and walked out of the room to have a cup of coffee.

Now I knew for sure that there was not that much depth to his knowledge of contemporary German. *Horchposten* is a Word War I term for a soldier who has to put his ear on the ground to try and detect movement in the opposing trenches. This is a form of surveillance, but it was totally unsuitable for the subject at hand.

Eventually, Walters was appointed ambassador to Bonn, and his German improved during his stay in Germany.

No matter how good your memory, there is no way of doing an accurate translation of a passage longer than five minutes only from memory. I did not believe the stories circulating in Washington that a few interpreters, like Vernon Walters, could actually do that and be complete and accurate. When President Georges Pompidou came to visit President Nixon, he got the full arrival ceremony on the South Lawn of the White House, even a Colonial fife and drum corps marching smartly by the leaders. I had heard from our senior French interpreter, Alec Toumayan, that Walters was going to do the welcoming speech instead of Alec.

For those ceremonies, you do not want any troublemakers in the welcoming crowd. Memoranda are circulated in government agencies like the State Department, asking for volunteers. I volunteered and stationed myself in the back of the crowd, half hidden by an overhanging bush.

When Nixon launched into his speech, sure enough, Walters was standing there, taking it all in by memory only. I pulled out my notebook and meticulously recorded the entire speech. Then Walters began. His French sounded good, and he spoke with clarity and conviction, except an entire sentence and parts of other sentences were missing, several things were changed around quite a bit, and a few words were added that the president never said. However, the main thrust and tenor were there. In fact, Walters's welcoming speech was a little better than Nixon's. Everybody was happy. He probably got a lot of praise for his interpreting. But if he had done this translation for an interpreter examining board at the State Department, his chances of passing the exam would have been slim.

GETTING KICKED OUT OF THE OVAL OFFICE

The occasional hostility of the White House toward State Department interpreters was enhanced by the isolation imposed on Secretary of State William Rogers by National Security Adviser Henry Kissinger and his staff. Some visits of foreign emissaries to the White House were kept confidential, and some incoming information from foreign countries was not passed on to the Department of State. The reasons I could not understand, because Rogers was an old and trusted friend of the president.

When interpreting for Rogers on matters concerning Germany, he had to turn to me every once in a while and ask for advice in a whisper. This was always on issues that the White House and I knew about, but he either had not been briefed on or had forgotten.

Once, I was called to the White House very late in the evening to interpret for a secret emissary of the German chancellor. He came alone, almost fully concealed by a trench coat and a broad-brimmed hat. I knew his identity, having interpreted for him before. Henry Kissinger and Helmuth Sonnenfeldt, the latter an expert on German and Soviet affairs on the National Security Council (NSC), were the American principals in the meeting. They understood the German well enough, so I interpreted only from English into German. When it was over, close to midnight, Sonnenfeldt ordered me to write a memorandum of the meeting immediately, bring the finished original back to the White House, and not to make a copy for anybody else.

To me, it made no sense to keep this information from Secretary Rogers, because the meeting concerned matters he was already involved with. I retreated to my office at the State Department and wrote the memorandum, making just one copy. Then I reasoned with myself. I was an employee of the Department of State, not of Helmuth Sonnenfeldt. The secretary of state was in charge of foreign policy and certainly entitled to this information. My standing State Department instructions were to leave the original of interpreting memoranda with the secretary's office and provide copies only to participants in the meeting. So that is what I did.

I took the elevator up to the Operations Center on the seventh floor and left the original memo there for the secretary. I put the copy in a sealed envelope for Sonnenfeldt and personally delivered it by taxi to the White House in the dead of night. The next day, I got a telephone call from Sonnenfeldt. Where was the original?

It was with Secretary Rogers, I told him and recited my standard instructions on such memoranda. "But we ordered you not to give a copy to anybody."

"I did not give a copy to anybody," I answered, "you have the only existing copy." It was too late for him to do anything about it, so he did not pursue the matter any further.

Maybe the above incident was the reason for what happened to me at the Oval Office a few months later. Former Chancellor Erhard was passing through Washington, returning from South America back to Germany. My German colleague Heinz Weber was traveling with him. I knew nothing about this until I got a call directly from the White House, asking me to come to the Oval Office to interpret a meeting between Nixon and Erhard. When I arrived, I joined the chancellor and Heinz in the Cabinet Room, waiting to be escorted into the Oval Office. The three of us were good friends by then and had a cordial greeting and chat while we were waiting.

When we were called into the president's office, I took a seat across from Nixon, so I could see his eyes and read his body language. Heinz was interpreting into English while I worked into German, our normal modus operandi. Suddenly, the other door to the Oval Office opened and Henry Kissinger walked in. He surveyed the scene and, without greeting the president, said to me, "You can go back to State, we keep Mr. Weber."

This not only surprised Erhard and Weber, it also puzzled me. The president had asked me to come to his office. How could Kissinger throw me out of it without asking the president's permission? I did not rise from my seat and threw a long, questioning glance at Nixon. The

president, always insecure, squirmed in his seat. He well understood what
my eyes were asking him: "Are you in charge here or Mr. Kissinger?"
After an awkward pause, he said softly, "I guess that would be all right.
We'll see you next time."

I got up and left. Professional interpreters do not fret much about
embarrassment. It is part of the job. But this time I was angry, because I
had been embarrassed in front of good friends and did not get a chance
to bid them good-bye after the meeting.

GETTING DRESSED DOWN FOR BEING DRESSED PROPERLY

When foreign dignitaries visit the United States, their visit revolves
around the arrangements made by the chief of protocol, located on
the first floor of what is now the Harry S. Truman Building, the
headquarters of the Department of State. President Nixon had appointed
Emil Mosbacher to this post. Mosbacher, a famous yachtsman from a
wealthy family, had won the America's Cup in 1962 and again in 1967,
but he had no experience in Washington protocol matters.

Mosbacher ran a tight ship at State, as he had done on the water. He
would not listen to advice and frustrated his staff no end. Protocol
officers who balked at his instructions were promptly fired. He also
would take no advice from interpreters on how the interpreting could
best be accomplished. Several of us, including me, had some tough
battles with him. He usually won the battles, but the interpreting often
suffered.

One warm summer day, I was sitting in my office at the State Department when the phone rang. It was Martin Hillenbrand, then director of the Office of Central European Affairs, which included Germany. He told me that German Chancellor Willy Brandt was on a private vacation in Florida and had just been invited to come over to Nixon's villa at Key Biscayne that afternoon. Mosbacher was already down there. He had ordered Martin and me to be at Key Biscayne in four hours for Brandt's arrival. "Meet me at the C-Street entrance in ten minutes. We need to rush to Andrews Air Force Base."

I grabbed an interpreting pad and two pens, told the front office where I was going, and went to the entrance. Hillenbrand was in his customary dark-blue pinstripe suit. Not expecting any high-level interpreting that day, I wore a light-blue summer suit. A small four-engine military jet was waiting to whisk us to Homestead Air Force Base near Miami, where a presidential helicopter scooped us up and dropped us on the lawn in front of Nixon's villa.

A few State Department and White House officials had formed a reception line on the lawn, as Brandt's helicopter was only a few minutes away. All, including Mosbacher, wore dark-blue suits and ties, uncomfortable in the hot and muggy air. Mosbacher immediately shot over to me and barked, "How dare you come dressed like this? You are sticking out like a sore thumb. Where is your dark suit?" I explained that I had had no warning and there had been no time to change. He was furious.

The chancellor's helicopter landed two minutes later. He stepped out in a light-blue suit with an open collar. The president stepped out of his villa, wearing a light beige summer suit and tie. I was the only one properly dressed. Ah, that sweet feeling of revenge.

A DARK FORTRESS SHIELDING
AN OLIGARCHY

When the1970s came around, I had been in the United States for a dozen years and had begun to understand and like the American concept of democracy, the great variety of people and ideas, the spirit of generosity and tolerance. Where things were not in order—the treatment of the black citizens, the poor, and the elderly—progress was being made, with much of the credit going to my first president, Lyndon Johnson, through his Great Society program.

The civil rights laws, Head Start, Medicare, and dozens of other remedial laws for what ailed the United States at that time had been passed by Congress in the sixties. Finally, there was new hope and optimism in the air after the assassinations of Martin Luther King, Jr. and the Kennedy brothers. My own spirits had been lifted by the many positive developments, despite the heavy cloud of Vietnam.

Even though I was just an interpreter, I was enmeshed in the emotional ups and downs of Washington. Under Johnson, I was usually treated warmly at the White House, where I had some interpreting business every month. I felt enveloped by the enthusiasm of LBJ when I had to relay his ideas to foreign leaders. It was fun sitting next to him. A visit to the Oval Office had become like a visit to a family living room.

With the arrival of Nixon, the White House had become a dark fortress. Even high-ranking officials in many government agencies, ours included, were afraid of the seemingly unchecked power of the oligarchy that now seemed to control everything: Henry Kissinger, Bob Haldeman, John Ehrlichman, and very few others.

We interpreters could not understand why Nixon and Kissinger preferred to have Victor Sukhodrev as the lone interpreter in many important talks with the Soviet Union. Victor is one of the most brilliant consecutive interpreters I have ever encountered. He and Heinz Weber were the two master interpreters whose level I was striving to reach as a journeyman. But Sukhodrev's father had been a Soviet spy in the United States for ten years. How could he be trusted more than an American interpreter with an impeccable record, such as William Krimer?

And who was monitoring him? One role of the second interpreter in such meetings is to monitor and assist his or her colleague. Even masters make mistakes or cannot come up with a critical term on the spur of the moment.

And who was writing the memorandum of conversation for our side? Victor?

Some of our interpreters were getting paranoid. When I made some critical remarks about something Nixon had done while having lunch with three colleagues at the department, they tried to hush me up. Somebody at the next table might be listening. I had risked my life to escape from East Germany, where one was not allowed to speak one's mind. Had the East German culture of fear and intimidation suddenly come to Washington?

Ever since my nine-day interpreting stint with Austrian Chancellor Klaus during his visit to the United States in 1968, I had become a trusted and popular interpreter with the Austrian leaders. In 1972, they had but one fully competent diplomatic interpreter for English in Vienna, and he was not always available. So, when Nixon was going to visit Austria in May 1972, the Austrian ambassador pleaded with me to accompany the president, knowing he often did not take American interpreters along. My superiors at State agreed and secured a seat for me on a White House staff plane to Salzburg.

The day before my departure, I was called into the office of Deputy Assistant Secretary John Condayan. He told me we had a problem. Somebody at the White House had just called him and told him I should not go to Salzburg, and that my seat on the plane had been given to somebody else. That somebody had also forbidden him to tell me who he was. I told John that we could not do that to the Austrians. It was the first time they had asked us for help. This made no sense. Somebody had to be there to interpret for both sides.

John held his hand over the telephone message pad so I could not read the name of the caller. But he held it in such a way that I could read the last three letters of the name: "man." He knew I would figure it out. I instantly knew that it was Bob Haldeman. Bucking Bob Haldeman in 1972 was extremely risky business. John knew that better than I. "You make the decision," he said. "If you go, I'll assist you best I can; if you don't, I fully understand why."

Without a moment's hesitation, I told him that I would go. Next, I went to see Chief Interpreter Donald Barnes; I told him what had occurred and that I was going. Don, who had never liked me very much, shook his head in disbelief. "It's been nice knowing you, Harry," he said with a sarcastic smile. "You obviously do not understand this town."

Condayan put me on a commercial plane to London, and I made my way to Salzburg. It turned out that I was very much needed in Austria. I did my job, flew back, and never heard a word about it from Bob

Haldeman. One year later, Haldeman was out of his job. But I still had mine.

I may not have liked Nixon very much and was sometimes put off by Kissinger's occasional rudeness and air of arrogance. But I had a great deal of admiration for their clear understanding of what China and the Soviet Union were all about and how to best deal with them.

When I was training interpreters at the Inlingua School of Interpretation in Arlington, Virginia, I often used excerpts from Nixon's book *The Real War*, especially from his chapter "World War III." It is one of the clearest and most cogent descriptions of what the Soviet system and the Soviet quest for world domination was all about.

I was always in awe of Henry Kissinger's ability to express the most complex thoughts so well in his writings in the English language, an acquired tongue for him, as for me. He had come to America from Bavaria, I came from Prussia. Prussians and Bavarians are ancient adversaries in German culture, also on the comedy circuit, where many jokes are cracked about these two German opposites. When Kissinger was appointed secretary of state and became my direct boss, I received two letters from Germany, asking how a Bavarian could become America's foreign minister ahead of a Prussian, when I had been at the State Department for so many years. The writers were joking, of course. I replied that there were two reasons. Kissinger was smarter than I, and he had met Nelson Rockefeller before I did. Without Rockefeller's generous support and sponsorship, Kissinger's career may have looked quite different. I later interpreted for and traveled with Rockefeller when he was Ford's vice president.

Kissinger's quick wit was refreshing. Once, after he had successfully concluded the Vietnam Peace Talks, a small group of us Americans were about to enter Claridge's Hotel in London. London, one of Kissinger's favorite cities, was just a quick stop on our way to Germany, but a few people knew that he was coming. A small group of Londoners were standing behind a police rope at the entrance to the hotel to catch a glimpse of Kissinger. He was walking directly in front of me when a portly matron leaned over the rope, almost blocking the secretary's path, and said to him very excitedly, "Thank you, Mr. Secretary! Thank you for saving the world!"

Kissinger stopped for two seconds, looked at her matter-of-factly, and responded, "You are welcome."

Only once, in the many years I worked for him, did Henry Kissinger make a positive personal remark to me. One day in the Oval Office, when I came up with a very felicitous solution for something that was difficult to translate from German into English, he turned his head to me and said, "That was brilliant. That was positively brilliant." I was pleasantly surprised. I never expected to hear that in the Nixon White House.

In his last two years in Washington, his command of German had been refurbished to the point that he could conduct even linguistically difficult meetings in German. But he still called me in many times to serve as a note taker, because his regular note takers could not understand German.

When the Watergate hearings dragged on about impeaching Nixon, and after Vice President Agnew had resigned, I had come to the conclusion that Nixon would resign rather than face an impeachment trial in the

Senate. When I told this to my colleagues at Language Services, it provoked laughter and derision. The American-born interpreters told me that, having come from Germany, I just did not understand the American political system. American presidents do not resign. None ever had. I felt put down and a little angry. So I offered to bet money on it.

After Nixon resigned, I walked around the office and collected $85 from my friends. A little vindication feels so good.

As he boarded *Air Force One* to depart Washington for California, Nixon turned and waved to the press and White House aides. He smiled and thrust his arms into the air as if in victory rather than defeat. Henry Kissinger made a long and pathetic farewell speech to the employees of the State Department. He was bitter and disappointed and made it sound as if his leaving this post would be a big loss for the department and U.S. foreign policy. But his star would soon rise again under President Ford.

PRESIDENTIAL VIGNETTES

GERALD R. FORD

1974–1977

FROM SALZBURG TO HELSINKI

For us interpreters, only one thing changed noticeably with the transition from Nixon to Ford. On entering the Oval Office, we were now greeted with a smile and an occasional firm handshake of the LBJ variety. No more icy stares and wrinkled eyebrows. Moreover, Jerry Ford knew several of us from his service as vice president and as minority leader in the House of Representatives, and we knew him as a forthright and warm person who was not given to double-talk and between-the-lines mysterious hints. Straight talk makes interpreting so much easier.

Even as vice president, he had been a welcome change from his predecessor, Spiro Agnew, who often had been arrogant and defiant in attitude and speech, although we delighted in some of his verbal creations, such as "nattering nabobs of negativism" or "effete corps of impudent snobs." Ford would never launch such poisonous arrows on anyone.

Ehrlichman and Haldeman were gone, but many others of Nixon's White House staff and most members of his cabinet stayed in place. The former staff members and the White House trip directors (who managed the logistics of his foreign travels) retained the attitude that interpreters were a nuisance rather than helpful members of the event team. Keeping us out of official photographs was foremost on their minds, and they often ignored our advice in the areas where we were experienced and they were not.

President Ford also decided to keep Henry Kissinger. This certainly made for a strange match. To Kissinger, the desired end often justified the means. He was wily, secretive, bending with the wind, and always scheming to find the best path to success. He would sometimes ignore or try to elbow out of the way people whom he saw as obstacles or who did not agree with his tactics or strategies. That made him a natural match for Nixon, who operated in a similar fashion. But Kissinger often seemed somewhat insecure in the presence of Nixon. From conversations that I interpreted where both were negotiating or speaking for the American side, I had the feeling that Nixon did not completely trust Kissinger, that he was sometimes monitoring Kissinger's remarks with a knitted brow and a suspicious eye. But then, Nixon was suspicious of everybody.

Ford's character was diametrically opposed to Kissinger's. His speech and thoughts were linear and without deception. He did not seem to have a mean bone in his body. In contrast to Nixon, Ford let Kissinger know that he fully trusted him and his judgment. Indeed, Ford admired Kissinger and would praise his intellect when speaking to others.

When interpreting meetings where both Ford and Kissinger were speaking for the American side, Kissinger seemed more relaxed and comfortable than with Nixon, and he asserted himself more, occasionally doing most of the talking. Ford did not mind that. He never gave him an annoyed or suspicious look, and virtually never corrected him.

MEETING ANWAR SADAT IN SALZBURG

A good example of the lack of knowledge of and experience with diplomatic interpreting on the part of White House aides and trip directors, and how the absence of that knowledge fails to serve the interests of the president, was evident when Ford went to Austria on June 1, 1975, for talks with President Anwar Sadat of Egypt. The trip director was Frank Ursomarso, a nice enough fellow, but not conversant with the logistics and intricacies of diplomatic interpreting.

I had first accompanied the president to a NATO meeting in Brussels. On that trip, I also met Colin Powell for the first time. He was along as a military adviser. Some of my colleagues had told me about his keen intellect and pleasant personality. I found this amply confirmed in Brussels. Little did I suspect that one day he would become chairman of the Joint Chiefs of Staff and eventually secretary of state.

From Brussels, Ford went to Madrid to meet with Generalissimo Francisco Franco, while I flew straight to Salzburg for his visit there the following day. When landing at the small airport, I remembered vividly what it had looked like when Nixon stopped in Salzburg in June of 1974. After all the American planes had landed, there was no room left to park the few arriving planes of Austrian Airlines. The huge wingspans of our military, staff, and press planes, and, finally, *Air Force One,* had

covered virtually the entire tarmac between the terminal building and
the taxiways. I was sure it would not be much different tomorrow.

When I returned to the airport the next day to interpret Ford's arrival
speech, it was pouring rain. I sought out Ursomarso to discuss the arrival
logistics with him. Much to my dismay, a separate set of microphones
had been set up for me, a good thirty feet from the spot where the
president would come down the stairs from *Air Force One* to be greeted
by Chancellor Bruno Kreisky and his entourage. Clearly, the only
reason for this was to keep me out of the range of the cameras that were
trained on the microphones to be used by Kreisky and Ford. Worse,
this put me behind the loudspeakers beamed at the press corps. How
would I be able to hear over the patter of the rain? I was too far away
to hear the president directly, and no loudspeaker was pointed in my
direction. We had a full hour to change things around, but Ursomarso
dismissed my protest with a cool smile. Everything would be just fine,
he assured me.

The president's plane stopped behind me. Looking to my right, I could
see him emerge from the cabin door and make his way down the
stairs. Then I could not see him anymore, because the umbrellas of
the welcoming party obscured my view. I whipped out my notebook
and waited for his voice. He started his arrival speech, and I could
barely hear what he said. The very first sentence puzzled me. He was
apologizing for something, but for what? He had just arrived in Austria.
What could he have done wrong so quickly? All I could hear after the
apology was a sound like "… umble …" I kept kicking this around in
my head while I took notes for the next sentences. Finally, I came to the
conclusion that he probably had said, "I apologize for the rain tumbling
down like that." So that is what I said in German.

The next morning, I picked up the *Salzburger Nachrichten* to read the local paper over breakfast. Three photos on the front page showed the sequence of Ford falling near the bottom steps as he was exiting his plane, and the Austrian chancellor and the military aide helping him back on his feet The headline above the photos read in German, "I apologize for stumbling into your country like that." Below the photos it complained, "The official interpreter of the president took no notice whatsoever of this remark." I was one of the very few at the airport who could not see the president fall.

A much worse logistics snafu happened during the evening banquet that Chancellor Kreisky gave for Presidents Ford and Sadat. The dinner would be closed to the press until the three leaders made remarks at the end of it. Then television cameras and reporters would be allowed in. Ursomarso told me to take the evening off and rest. I would not be needed at the banquet because Kreisky and Sadat could speak English.

"How about the toasts?" I asked.

"We have spoken to the Austrian and Egyptian protocol people. Sadat and Kreisky will make their remarks in English."

"Wait a minute, Frank. You cannot rely on promises from protocol people. The leaders can do what they want. Austrian radio and television are here. The chancellor may prefer to speak in German. If he does, Sadat may respond in German, because he speaks German quite well. Radio Cairo is here. Sadat may even speak in Arabic and have arranged for a translation into German. That is not going to help President Ford any. If I am there, I can put the German into English for him."

Ursomarso was unmoved. I told him I did not need a seat at the table, but I should definitely be in the room, close to the president.

"Trust me. Everything will work out all right."

I was denied access to the banquet hall and went to another room in the building to watch the dinner speeches on Austrian television.

Chancellor Kreisky spoke first—in German. Poor Jerry Ford could not understand anything except the mention of his name. Then Sadat rose and spoke—a few words in Arabic and mostly in German. President Ford had to sit there without knowing what Sadat was saying, although the American taxpayers had financed my trip to Salzburg to assist him. Then Ford took the microphone and had to make his dinner speech without any chance to refer to the remarks of the other two leaders or to thank them for the compliments paid him and his country.

I went to bed angry. Surely, next morning people would ask me, not Ursomarso, why I had not been there to help our president. If Ford ever complained about it, I was not made aware of it. But if this had happened to Lyndon Johnson, there would have been hell to pay.

Much to my regret, I never attended any of the meetings that President Sadat had in Austria with Nixon and Ford. Both times, I was there for our meetings with the Austrian leaders. Anwar Sadat was a highly interesting and fascinating person. Nixon and Ford came from families of modest means. Sadat spent most of his childhood in poverty. His father had thirteen children to support on a modest salary. Sadat learned English and German from other inmates in British jails in Egypt, where he was imprisoned for fighting the British. He became one of the greatest leaders modern Egypt ever had, a man of courage and a man of peace who hated to spill blood, even the enemy's blood.

THE HELSINKI FINAL ACT

The thirty-five-nation Conference on Security and Cooperation in Europe, after two years of intensive negotiations, had agreed on a set of documents, dubbed the Helsinki Accords. They were to be signed in Finland on August 1, 1975.

The conference was the result of two different foreign-policy goals. The goal of the Soviet Union, having absorbed by force virtually all the nations in Eastern Europe after World War II, was to try to get official recognition of the de-facto postwar borders, especially the new borders around Poland and the one dividing once mighty Germany into two states: one free and democratic, called the Federal Republic of Germany, the other not free and not democratic, called—what else?—the German Democratic Republic. After World War II, no peace treaty had ever been signed with Germany.

The goal of the other side in the cold war, the free nations, was to incorporate into the agreement the recognition of individual rights and other liberties by the thirty-five signatories, through having the Communist despotic regimes put their signatures under an extensive vocabulary of such rights that existed only in the hearts and minds of the suppressed people, but could not be practiced in those Soviet-controlled states. Just the mention of them could cost citizens prison terms or even their lives.

By allowing open discussion of these subjects in the Soviet-controlled sphere, as well as monitoring compliance with the Helsinki Final Act within that sphere, it was hoped that ultimately the genie of individual freedom would escape from the tightly corked Communist bottle. History has shown that this approach worked and has vindicated its proponents, such as the German statesman and visionary Hans-Dietrich Genscher, often vilified in the seventies for selling out German reunification by promoting recognition of the postwar borders including the one between the two Germanys. This recognition turned out to be temporary and a first step leading to the eventual erasure of that border and German reunification in 1989.

Disregarding certain reservations by Henry Kissinger and, even more so, by Helmut Sonnenfeldt of the National Security Council, President Ford unequivocally supported the Helsinki Accords and did not buy into the notion that the Baltic states were by now an "organic part of the Soviet Union." Years later, Ford claimed that the human rights part of the final act had prepared the path for the events of 1989, and he professed pride in having signed it.

But before the act could be signed on August 1, 1975, the six different language versions of the draft had to be compared and certified by linguistic experts to be saying the same in each language.

GENEVA

Certifying that bilingual or multilingual agreements have the same meaning in each individual sentence is a step all nations take before signing them. In the United States, this task also falls to the Office of

Language Services at the Department of State. Only after the director of that office has signed off that the language versions are in substantive conformity will the president or the secretary of the appropriate federal department affix their signature to the agreement.

For the Helsinki Accords, the certification teams of the thirty-five nations were to meet in Geneva in early July for what was estimated to be about five to seven days of language comparison work.

In 1975, the managers at Language Services felt that I had the most exposure to the contemporary German of both German states. I had been the interpreter for the first official U.S. delegation ever to negotiate in East Germany in 1973 and had been back to East Berlin a few more times. I had a solid grounding in the finer points of the German spoken and written in the Federal Republic and in Austria. In addition, I was one of the few diplomatic interpreters who held a degree in written translation (from the University of Mainz) and had done some difficult agreement translations for the U.S. government.

That appeared to make me the logical choice as the lead certifier for German. Language Services also sent top linguists for the other four foreign languages. Our largest group was for German and Russian, because we expected that most objections would come from the Soviet Union and East Germany, the two countries most interested in watering down their language versions to camouflage some of their concessions, especially on human rights. This assumption proved to be right on the money.

Diplomatic interpreters travel constantly and can pack a suitcase quickly if they know where they are going, for what purpose, and for how long. You do not have to be dressed up sitting in a translating office, but you need a suit and tie for dinners and receptions. Thus, I was packed in twenty minutes for seven days in summery Geneva. Little did I know when I touched down in Switzerland that this would come back to haunt me later.

The conference certification subcommittee for German, in which mostly East German objections were raised, consisted of Austria, East and West Germany, Luxemburg, Liechtenstein, and Switzerland. Those objections and suggestions for compromises were then passed on to our team that was part of the English certification group. By fortunate happenstance, the head of the German language subcommittee was Klaus Merten, a former fellow student at the Germersheim campus of Mainz University, now a German diplomat. We had not seen each other in nineteen years. He kept me fully informed on every little intrigue happening in his committee.

Day by day, the objections in the Russian and German subcommittees kept piling up. Time and again, the unfortunate linguists from the Soviet Union and Communist East Germany were proven wrong by the language experts from the other countries. Their suggestions did not reflect the same meaning as the wording in the English, French, and other drafts, but they rarely would compromise. It was clear that they were under political instructions to try and incorporate fuzzy and misleading language into the Russian and German version of the accords. By Friday of the first week, no end was in sight for the many disputes. Washington extended our travel orders for a second week.

During the second week, Klaus Merten invited me to come to the delegation headquarters of the Federal Republic of Germany in the Rue de Lausanne. He told me that the subcommittee had approved a few suggestions that I had formulated. I should come and work directly in the German subcommittee and table my suggestions immediately rather than sending them back and forth between committees. It would save time. I responded that I would be glad to do that, but that it might help me if I could sit in for at least a day on the plenary meetings of the political negotiators. This might allow me to get a reading as to whether the language comparison strategy of the Soviets and East Germans was to torpedo the signing of the final act on August 1 or whether they just wanted to use as much time as possible in July to get their texts watered down.

I had already made this request to the head of the American delegation, but he would not issue or loan me a badge to enter the conference room. Those badges, he said, were just for delegates, not for translators. Klaus was a more practical diplomat. A German delegate had been unable to come to Geneva, but his credentials were in his desk drawer.

"You are now Dr. Fuchs from the Federal Republic when you wear this. I'll cover for you if necessary. Stay in the back of the room and do not get involved in talking with other delegates. Just listen to the discussions for a couple of days. Then give me back the credentials."

Two or three times during the next two days, I sat in the back of the plenary and listened to the Communist delegations. I came away with the impression that they were not planning to prevent the signing on August 1. Merten shared my opinion. I suggested that we needed to throw the East German linguists some bones. They were constantly outvoted in Merten's committee, because linguistically they were usually wrong, and there was no other Communist country in that committee to vote with them.

"Let us not give ground on language of substantive importance," I suggested, "but let them put in some of their strange suggestions where nothing of substance is compromised. They need to report some acceptances by the committee to save their jobs and their necks, and their political bosses need to cable some successes to East Berlin."

Klaus agreed with this strategy, and we brought other committee members on board. For instance, in the subject area of libraries and motion pictures, the East Germans had drafted some words that had drifted into East German usage directly from Russian. None of the other German-speaking countries used these words, thus they were not found in their drafts. Conversely, most educated speakers of German would readily understand what was meant by those terms.

As suggested by Merten, I joined his subcommittee and sat at the table with the other linguists. After the majority of the committee had twice voted to adopt suggestions I made at the table, the senior East German reviewer protested my presence, because the United States was not an official member of that committee. Klaus retorted that I was not there officially, but had been invited by him, the chairman, to join as a language consultant. The East German would not budge and insisted that I leave the room or they would.

Once again, Klaus showed his diplomatic skills. He agreed that under the rules I could not be there and personally escorted me out of the room into the corridor. He pointed to a window seat and said, "Harry, please just sit down there with your briefcase and read the newspaper. Whenever we need your help, I will send somebody outside. That same person can then carry your suggestion inside to the discussion table." We worked like that for a couple of days and let the East Germans have some small victories. By Friday, though, it was clear that a third week was needed to get agreement, mostly on Russian and German language issues. Washington extended our travel orders again.

At the end of the third week, a cable came from the State Department for me with a set of new travel orders. President Ford was going to pay an official visit to Germany before going on to Helsinki. I was to go from Switzerland directly to Bonn and then on to Finland. Having packed for only one week of text comparisons in Geneva now came back to haunt me. My wardrobe was not suitable for the presidential visit. In addition to other formal events, President Walter Scheel was going to give a black-tie dinner for President and Mrs. Ford. The stores in Geneva were closed for the weekend. I would not be able to rent a tuxedo in Bonn on a Sunday. I called the State Department Office of Operations in Washington and explained my problem.

The U.S. Air Force came to the rescue. Every day, a plane or two left Andrews Air Force Base near Washington for Frankfurt or some other field in Germany. A military aide picked up my tuxedo, shirts, ties, and cufflinks from our house, and my clothes were sent across the Atlantic within hours. Everything was waiting for me by the time I arrived in Bonn.

JERRY FORD'S MOSQUITO AND THE SHARPSHOOTERS

When going to Europe with the president, it is usually an overnight flight across the Atlantic. The interpreters arrive tired and have to dig deep into their stamina to make it through a long and difficult first day of public and private meetings and events. This time, I had come to Bonn from Geneva, well rested but totally unprepared. I spent most of my free evening reading the available briefing books and studying the events schedule given to me by our embassy in nearby Bad Godesberg.

When I was finished reading the voluminous material, it was past midnight. Before going to bed, I made one more stop in the control room in our hotel to check my slot for messages. The control room, usually bustling, was now quiet. Only three typists were there, pecking away at their typewriters. A tall gentleman walked in, looking exhausted. He checked his message slot and asked out aloud, "Is anybody still up who can help me with writing speeches? There is so much left to do."

Although I did not know who he was, I introduced myself and asked if there was any way I could help. He said he was Milton Friedman. Knowing that much of our political agenda with Germany and other countries dealt with economics, I was impressed that the president had brought a famous economist with him. I told Friedman that I had read a lot about him.

"No, no," he chuckled. "I am a White House speechwriter with the same name, not an economics expert." He gave the secretaries a text to type. Then we retreated to his room.

While I was drafting a couple of paragraphs on Berlin for him, he was working on a passage for Ford's remarks to be given at President Scheel's upcoming black-tie dinner aboard the pleasure ship *Drachenfels* while cruising the Rhine.

Friedman was moaning to me, "Why is the Rhine flowing from south to north when I have to fit the river into a paragraph dealing with East-West relations?"

I looked at him and volunteered, "When a river flows from south to north, are the bridges not leading to the east and to the west?"

"Bingo! Why didn't I think of that?" he responded.

I went to bed at 2:00 am feeling sorry for him, who was far from finished with his work.

After three stifling hot and humid weeks in Geneva, Bonn offered no relief. Having to move around in dark suits and ties during an official visit made it even more uncomfortable. On July 27, 1975, after a meeting with Chancellor Helmut Schmidt, the six participants in that meeting—President Ford, Chancellor Schmidt, Hans-Dietrich Genscher, Henry Kissinger, and the two interpreters, Gisela Siebourg and I—were standing in the garden of the chancellery on the open lawn for an outdoor press conference. We men were all in dark suits and white shirts. Gisela wore a white dress.

The Rhine was not far away. On the banks of that famous river lives a particularly nasty breed of mosquito, called *schnake* in the local parlance. When I was enrolled in translation studies at the Germersheim campus of Mainz University in the mid-fifties, I had become thoroughly acquainted with this mosquito. The Germersheim campus is also near the Rhine. In summer, we used to take girlfriends down to the river to sunbathe with them on towels or blankets. The mosquitoes, usually preferring hot and humid days, would land on our exposed skin so skillfully that we did not know they were there until they stung us. They did not like superficial stings, but would bore deep to drink our blood. Their stings were painful.

Being smart college students, we used the mosquitoes to our advantage. Keeping our eyes riveted to all exposed skin areas of the girls, we would keep mosquito watch. Once landed, they usually could not be made to leave by just waving your hand at them. You had to pick them off. This allowed us to touch the girls without having to ask permission. Of course, we were just being gallant knights.

So, on this humid August day in Bonn, the six of us were standing on the chancellor's lawn. Schmidt was making a statement into the microphones. I was standing behind Ford's right shoulder, whispering a translation. The other three were standing a step back behind us. When we had taken up our positions in front of the press and the television cameras a little earlier, I had noticed two or three German sharpshooters, part of the tight security for the event, on the roof of the building to our right. Their telescopic guns were aimed right at our group.

Too busy with my simultaneous interpreting, I had not noticed that a schnake had landed on the back of the president's suit, because it was black on black. But I suddenly saw it appear on his white collar. I knew what would happen next, once it got the scent of the former football player's skin. It briefly flapped its wings and landed silently on his neck. My natural instinct was to pick it off before the president got stung.

But then I remembered the sharpshooters. I was in their direct line of sight, with nobody standing to my right. If I made a quick move for the neck of the president of the United States of America, one of them might just pull the trigger. Like interpreters, sharpshooters make decisions in split seconds. Like interpreters, they sometimes make the wrong decision. I quickly folded both of my hands behind my back. Then I saw Jerry Ford wince, but he remained standing rigidly upright, a brave and stalwart athlete.

I kept quiet about my cowardice until I told the truth to my German colleague, Heinz Weber, a few weeks later. Heinz searched through the Foreign Office photo archives until he found a picture showing Ford wince and me staring at his neck. He mailed a copy to me in Washington. I always felt a little guilty about my selfishness. The odds of me getting shot by one of those sharpshooters were probably six to one in my favor. After all, most people survive playing Russian roulette.

The mosquito sting at an outdoor press conference in Bonn. From left: Henry Kissinger, Gisela Siebourg (German interpreter), Foreign Minister Genscher, Obst, President Ford, Chancellor Schmidt. *Photo courtesy of German Foreign Office*

THE HELSINKI SUMMIT OF
THIRTY-FIVE NATIONS

After his visit to Germany, President Ford flew to Poland, where I was not needed. This gave me the opportunity to go to Finland ahead of him. I had never been there before and tried to learn a few words of the Finnish language. The only language Finnish is remotely related to is Hungarian. I did not know a word of Hungarian. Having no associations to work with in my head, learning a few phrases and words in Finnish proved to be extremely difficult. I was still hard at work on this when I was on a Lufthansa flight from Frankfurt to Helsinki.

After four weeks of the stifling heat and humidity in Switzerland and Germany, I was looking forward to the cool air of Finland. It was not to happen. The temperature on my arrival was in the high eighties and the humidity was at 90 percent. That was my first disappointment. When I arrived at my hotel, the venerable Kalastajatorppa, looking out on the Gulf of Finland in a beautiful setting, I discovered that it had no air-conditioning. The temperature in my room was in the low nineties, even with the windows open. The higher-ranking members of the American delegation were staying at the Hesperia, closer to the conference site, Finlandia Hall. The Hesperia, only three years old in 1975, was air-conditioned, a great blessing in those blazing July days.

After checking in with the embassy, I took a stroll down Mannerheim Boulevard to get a feel for the city. Everything was modern, clean, and reflecting a country of prosperity. Virtually all the women I encountered were strikingly beautiful, the men trim and handsome. Most everybody spoke some English, making my meager knowledge of Finnish unnecessary. Knowing that sleeping in this heat would be a challenge, I had only a sardine sandwich and chilled lemonade for dinner.

At midnight, the temperature in my room was still in the eighties, the humidity stifling. At 1:30, though tired, I still could not fall asleep. Frustrated, I put on some clothes, strung my voluminous conference credentials around my neck, and set out for a walk by the bay. The hotel was heavily guarded. As I made my way down to a path following the immediate shoreline, two young soldiers with submachine guns followed me. They trailed along on a second path in the trees on the slope above, as I was walking along the edge of the water. It was a trifle cooler by the bay than in my room, but there was no breeze. I found a rock to sit on, took off my shoes and socks, and dangled my feet in the water. My eyes searched the dark bay and traced the familiar stars above. Except for the sound of the night animals and the water, everything was quiet.

Suddenly, a strange feeling came over me. First, a shiver ran down my spine, as if I had seen a ghost or a frightening shadow. Then a feeling of great tranquility, inner peace, and contentment swept aside my frustrations and the discomfort of the heat. Had I fallen asleep and was dreaming? With the plaintive croaking of a frog, the explanation finally came to me.

This was the night scent, these were the night sounds of my native East Prussian coast, 600 miles to the southwest across the Baltic Sea. The smell of the birches, the willows, the reeds in the water felt pleasant and familiar. I had not been back in this area in thirty-one years. Yet the land and the sea were still speaking to me. They had been home to generations of my family before me. I was tied to the land and the sea by an invisible and strong bond. Much to the dismay of the soldiers above, I stayed in place and savored that feeling for another half hour. Then I put socks and shoes back on my wet feet and returned to the Kalastajatorppa. Sleep finally came to me.

HELLO, VICTOR!

In the afternoon of the first conference day, there was an outdoor cocktail reception for the members of the thirty-five delegations on a wide, sweeping lawn. The road went by the upper edge of the lawn. More than a hundred dignitaries and staff and their Finnish hosts were swarming over the lawn, cocktail glasses or lemonade in hand. President Ford and Leonid Brezhnev were yet to arrive. The Soviet lead interpreter, Victor Sukhodrev, the darling of Richard Nixon and Henry Kissinger, who had often let him interpret alone at the exclusion of the American White House interpreters, was hanging around close to the road, expecting Brezhnev's Zil limousine to show up. I did the same, waiting for Ford's mighty armored Lincoln Continental, because the chancellors of Austria and Germany were in the crowd.

The Lincoln arrived first. Gerald Ford, his wife Betty, and their son Jack climbed out of the car and gazed across the lawn, trying to spot a familiar dignitary to walk over to and greet. Finally, Ford saw a familiar face. He made a beeline for Sukhodrev and greeted him boisterously with "Hello, Victor!" He introduced Betty and Jack, and had a long conversation with him. A bunch of prime ministers and presidents were casting jealous glances in the direction of Sukhodrev. Many of them were still strangers to Jerry Ford, but Victor was an established fixture on the American diplomatic stage.

When a similar outdoor reception was held on the grounds of the Kalastajatorppa on Thursday evening, hosted by interim Prime Minister Keijo Liinamaa, the Finnish coast guard spotted a private motorboat without lights approaching across the bay. A patrol boat zoomed out of the hotel jetty and signaled the boat to stop and heave-to. When the boat did not respond, a coast guard officer fired a tracer shell toward it. The shell scored a direct hit on a vulnerable part of the boat, and it burst into flames. The two occupants were killed. They were locals who probably had had too much to drink. The coast guard men were also accused of having been inebriated and firing with poor aim. They were later tried and punished.

President Ford speaks at a military picnic in Germany. Interpreter Obst takes notes, next to German Minister of Defense Leber at the back of the platform. *Photo courtesy of German Foreign Office*

In Helsinki, I was not just assisting the president but also other members of the American delegation, primarily Henry Kissinger. This meant going in and out of the Hesperia Hotel, where our control room was, and in and out of the conference site, the huge Finlandia Hall. I enjoyed this, not because of the work, but because these two buildings were an air-conditioned refuge from the brutal heat, for me and for others (19,000 bottles of soda and beer were consumed at Finlandia Hall alone during the three days of the conference).

One afternoon, I found myself alone in an elevator of the Hesperia, going down to the lobby. The door opened on one floor. In walked Josip Broz Tito, in his marshal's uniform and without a bodyguard. He avoided eye contact with me, propped himself against the back wall, and stared straight ahead. I had never seen the eighty-three-year-old dictator before, so I was rattled by his appearance. His face was waxen and completely unnatural. He looked like he had just walked out of Madame Tussaud's Wax Museum or returned from a visit to a taxidermist. His wooden and stiff posture compounded that impression.

While I was still studying his face, looking for a sign of life, the door opened again. Archbishop Makarios, the leader of Cyprus, entered in flowing robes, full of life and flashing a smile. This made Tito, who also would not look at Makarios, seem even more dead. Getting no attention from the Yugoslav and seeing the American credentials on my chest, Makarios nodded slightly in my direction and said in English, "Good afternoon!"

Taken by surprise, I could not remember by what title an archbishop needed to be addressed. So, I responded simply, "Good afternoon, sir." Then we reached the lobby. My only close-up encounter with these two famous men was over.

One day, I was checking my in-box in the control room and found that I was scheduled to interpret a meeting between Kissinger and the Hungarian foreign minister. I was in shock because my Hungarian, like my Finnish, was nonexistent. It turned out that the minister had once studied in Germany and had a fair command of the German language. We had no interpreter for Hungarian with us, so we did the meeting in German. Such meetings are always difficult for the interpreter because you are not familiar with the names of the people, places, and institutions in those countries, plus you usually know very little about their national policies and problems. I remembered a similar meeting with the finance minister of Afghanistan, where I thought *"afghani"* referred to the people in that country when, instead, it referred to the currency. Fortunately, the meeting with the Hungarian did not cause me a similar embarrassment.

FEASTING WHILE THE PRESIDENT IS SUFFERING

It was quite an event for small Finland to be hosting the leaders of thirty-five nations at the same time. It was a feather in the cap of President Urho Kekkonen, then seventy-five years old. He looked bigger and stronger than even the former football player Jerry Ford and was just exuding confidence and energy during the conference.

The biggest social event was a banquet in the Presidential Palace.

I arrived early and studied the seating plan. President Ford was seated between Austrian Chancellor Kreisky on his right and East German Prime Minister Erich Honecker on his left. This immediately worried me. Kreisky and Ford knew each other well, but Honecker had never spoken with an American president. We had only established diplomatic relations with the German "Democratic" Republic the previous September. Honecker, not known for subtle diplomacy, would be eager to be seen talking to Ford on television and before the eyes of all the other leaders. He likely would be all over our president with nonstop talk, and Ford was not knowledgeable on the GDR.

Under the circumstances, I saw it as part of my task to bring Kreisky into the conversation as much as possible to allow the president to enjoy this banquet and not have to defend himself against a constant political mosquito attack from his left. I had a folding chair at my disposal and placed it behind and between Honecker and Ford as soon as the president sat down. No sooner had I sat down, when two prime ministers needed to pass us to get to their seats farther to the left. I got up, pushed the chair in a little, and stepped back under a decorative rubber tree to let them get by. That obscured my vision for just four or five seconds. When the two had passed, an East German interpreter was sitting in my chair. He must have hidden behind another rubber tree and shot out like a bullet.

When I told him that he was sitting in my chair, he just gave me an icy stare. Honecker was just starting to speak to Ford, and the East German began to interpret into English.

Like Honecker, I had noticed that the television cameras, now that Ford had arrived, were trained on our group. I could not possibly start a quarrel with another interpreter in plain view of the whole world. Grimly, I realized that I had been outsmarted and outmaneuvered. There was no place for me to sit or even to stand unobtrusively and interpret. The president would be suffering a verbal onslaught, and I could not help him.

I gritted my teeth, stepped off the stage, and left the banquet hall. As I was pacing up and down in the marble corridor, the Finnish chief of protocol caught up with me. He praised me for my restraint and for not making a scene on television. Then he asked me to follow him. We went down a side corridor. "You will be the only interpreter who can eat and drink tonight," he said with a smile. He opened a door and led me to a small table. Seated there were the president's physician and his military aide. I became the third American at the table.

Still angry, I briefly told them what had happened. I was hoping one of them might pass this on to Ford, who must have wondered why I had deserted him like that. Finally, I settled down to reindeer meat and an excellent red wine that helped to calm me down, until my foot hit something under the table. It was the black briefcase of the military aide, who quickly pulled it closer to him. My God, that was the briefcase with the nuclear code. Buried in it was the potential death of millions of people. For the second time in Helsinki, a shiver ran down my spine. I finally got to eat and drink, but I did not completely enjoy it.

Interpreting at Economic Summits

Origin of the Summits

The idea of holding annual economic "summits" grew out of a meeting of four men in the library of the White House on March 25, 1973, and a second meeting of two of them in Helsinki in August of 1975. In 1973, George Shultz was secretary of the treasury. His British colleague Tony Baker, Helmut Schmidt of Germany, who had just switched portfolios from defense to finance, and the French finance minister, Valery Giscard d'Estaing, were the other three. Before appearing in a public forum, the four had agreed to discuss in private what could be done about the turmoil in the world financial systems caused by a huge spike in oil prices.

The meeting was a success, and the four wanted to continue such private discussions in the future. This "Library Group" or "Group of Four" soon became the "Group of Five" by adding the finance minister of Japan. By 1975, two of the original four, Schmidt and Giscard d'Estaing, had been elected chiefs of government of Germany and France. Both attended the thirty-five-nation meeting in Helsinki to sign the Final Act of the Conference on Security and Cooperation in Europe. In the sweltering heat that had gripped Europe in July of 1975 and kicked the temperature and humidity in Finland up to Houston, Texas, levels, an idea the two had discussed earlier was agreed on during a garden conversation between Giscard d'Estaing and Schmidt. Why not have such meetings at the chiefs of government level, have the ministers of finance and foreign affairs sit in, and call them "summits"?

The French president immediately took the initiative and hosted the first such summit in November of 1975 at the Chateau Rambouillet near Paris. The president of the council of ministers of Italy was also invited. Aldo Moro accepted, making it the "Group of Six." In 1976, Canada joined. This new constellation of the "Group of Seven," or simply "G7," prevailed until the Twenty-Third Economic Summit, held by President Clinton in Denver in 1997, when the president of the Russian Federation was added, making it the "G8."

In the 1970s and 1980s, the constellation of the "Group of Seven Industrialized Nations" was roughly representative of the economic and financial powerhouses of the world. The composition heavily favored Europe, furnishing five of the eight participants: the presidents of France and the European Commission (added in 1977 but not representing a nation, thus still the Group of Seven), the prime ministers of Italy and the United Kingdom, and the chancellor of the Federal Republic of Germany, representing the free and economically vibrant part of divided Germany. In later years, the gravitational field of the world economy shifted in other directions. Countries like China, India, Russia, Brazil, and South Korea became big players in production and consumption.

Once the chiefs of government had an opportunity to be together each spring or summer, other topics were brought up for discussion that had little to do with economics or finance. The summits also opened the door to on-site bilateral meetings of any two of the leaders. A three-tier format developed under which chiefs of government, foreign ministers, or finance ministers hold separate parallel meetings, complicating the procedures and logistics, especially for language support.

A FORMIDABLE CHALLENGE FOR INTERPRETERS AND TRANSLATORS

Interpretation and translation are important operational components of these summits, especially interpretation. Teams of fifty to eighty interpreters and translators are needed for the smooth functioning of the two- or three-day annual event. As the meetings often operate on three separate tiers, although two or three of them may meet together occasionally, each tier needs interpreters. The three principals to be assisted for the United States are the president, the secretary of state, and the secretary of the treasury.

The meetings produce or present papers in different languages for discussion. Many of these must be translated immediately, sometimes overnight, requiring highly skilled translators. Occasionally, interpreters are kept up late into the night to supplement the translators to meet urgent deadlines. Often these papers are drafted by the "sherpas." Each participating government names a sherpa well ahead of the meeting. They meet long before and again during the summits, shape the agenda and the discussion papers, and prepare and guide their leaders. The original purpose of putting these meetings into the hands of the sherpas was to bypass the involvement of the national bureaucracies in order to provide for some privacy and expediency.

Usually three teams of simultaneous interpreters are required, covering English, French, German, Italian, Japanese, and now Russian. The country hosting the meeting provides and pays for all simultaneous interpreters and for the translators. These interpreters need to be well versed in economic and financial matters. Assembling enough of them is a major headache for the person in charge of language support, because those few top specialists are in demand for other organizations and meetings. The simultaneous interpreters constantly have to watch out for the common traps in the heat of split-second interpretation. For instance, American trillions are billions in German, and the German milliards are American billions. The British prefer one thousand millions, and so on. The team serving the chiefs of government invariably gets exposed to political and other issues as well.

For the bilateral meetings of the leaders or their ministers, highly skilled consecutive interpreters are required, with each delegation bringing their own from the home country. Like state funerals, economic summits furnish an opportunity for the top diplomatic interpreters of each country to get acquainted, socialize, and talk shop. In contrast to most diplomatic meetings and visits by leaders to other countries, during which diplomatic interpreters hardly ever get to eat or sleep, here the scene is much more peaceful for them.

Although the simultaneous interpreters are in constant motion, the typical bilateral interpreter handles only a few hours of consecutive interpreting during a summit, leaving ample private time to observe the discussions and learn from them, not only the terminology but how the economic and financial world operates at the strategic level, what is important, and what is secondary. I was always fascinated by the amount of knowledge I was privileged to accumulate without studying the subject at a university. Having attended about a dozen summits in one capacity or another, I would not want to have missed any one of them. It was at economic summits that I finally had an opportunity to have a private chat with such famous diplomatic interpreters as Ken Yokota of Japan and Christopher Thiery of Paris.

SUMMIT EXPERIENCES

PUERTO RICO 1976

President Gerald Ford had agreed to host the Second Economic Summit in June of 1976. I do not know whether the selection of the site had anything to do with the president's love of golf, but it took place at two resort hotels in Dorado Beach, Puerto Rico. Apart from looking out on the Atlantic, the resort sported a beautiful golf course. The U.S. delegation was staying at the smaller Dorado Beach Hotel, a collection of private villas and low-rise buildings. The other delegations shared the more modern high-rise Cerromar Beach Hotel, a short walk away.

As my mind flashes back, I remember big lizards running through the lobby at will and the contents of the suitcase of one of my female staff colleagues being unceremoniously dumped on the lawn by Secret Service agents, who were rifling through her underwear in search of something suspicious. I also remember Chancellor Schmidt getting off a helicopter, wearing a Hamburg sea captain's cap as he stepped into the subtropical sun with a big smile.

Gerald Ford was a gracious and well-liked host. A couple of times, he had outdoor lunches set up when sudden rain arrived and everything had to be hustled inside in a matter of seconds. It was the most relaxed and friendly summit I can remember, not only for the politicians but also for the interpreters.

Early one morning, a few of us American interpreters were swimming in the small lagoon in front of the hotel, getting in a little relaxation and exercise before the morning meetings started. Suddenly, a curious sight approached. Canadian Prime Minister Pierre Elliot Trudeau was running along the beach, clad only in his swimming trunks. Two security agents in dark suits and ties, lugging weapons and communications gear, were running behind him, sweating profusely and trying to keep up. Much to their relief, Trudeau plunged into the lagoon when he spotted us and swam over to our group. He started a conversation with us, mostly directed at staff interpreter Sophia Porson, who was not only attractive but also fluent in French, English, and Portuguese. Trudeau, bilingual himself, had always shown great respect for interpreters and their work.

This ten-minute meeting in the lagoon accrued to our benefit five years later when Trudeau was hosting the Seventh Summit in Montebello and Ottawa; he treated the entire language team to a reception with smoked sturgeon, good wine, and musical entertainment. Before Clinton arrived on the scene, he was easily the most laid-back and informal chief of government I had ever encountered.

BONN 1978

The economies of the G7 nations had been rocked by steep increases in world oil prices, precipitating rises in unemployment and inflation. The Bonn Summit devoted much of its time to the question of energy policies. President Carter had just completed a very successful trip to other parts of West Germany and Berlin, during which I had interpreted four speeches in the consecutive mode and one town meeting in simultaneous. The enthusiastic reception he had received in Berlin had put him in a buoyant mood, and he had prepared an uplifting concluding statement for the end of the summit, when each leader was supposed to read such a statement on live television from a prepared text that would made available to the interpreters for simultaneous interpretation, carried by radio and television into many countries.

By this time, I had developed a more relaxed and confident working relationship with Germany's top English interpreter, Heinz Weber, having become an experienced and more polished diplomatic interpreter myself. During this summit, I was in a good mood because the concluding sentence I had written for Carter's keynote speech at the Berlin Airlift Memorial on July 15 (*Was immer sei, Berlin bleibt frei!*) had been the headline in many German newspapers the following morning, instantly earning me compliments from several American and German diplomats.

For some reason, Heinz had the text of Carter's concluding statement before I had seen it. The statement also had to be translated in written form into German and the other summit languages for distribution to the press at the concluding session. Heinz telephoned me to ask my help with an unanticipated problem with Carter's text.

Jimmy Carter, a great advocate for human rights and the cause of freedom, was quoting eight lines from a poem by Friedrich Schiller in his text. Schiller, whose *Ode to Joy* forms the scintillating finale to Beethoven's Ninth Symphony (now also the anthem of the United Nations), had become one of Carter's favorite poets. A great admirer of

Schiller myself, I was not aware of this before Heinz told me. The problem was that Carter's statement did not name the poem from which the lines were extracted. Not a single interpreter or translator in Bonn that day had been able to trace the poem from the English lines. In Germany, the original Schiller lines were needed. An approximate translation might provoke ridicule or nasty press reports. Could I help?

I had Weber read me the lines twice over, but remained puzzled. A distant bell in my memory said "*Die Horen*," but I was not at all sure. *Die Horen* was also the title of a literary magazine of that period. Maybe I was mixing things up. Several of us got on the telephone and called up professors of literature at the universities. Nobody could solve the puzzle.

With time running out, we decided that I might want to try and translate the lines into Schillerian German myself; I knew the writing style of the poet and had written poems in German myself since the 1950s. Maybe I could come close. If even the literature professors could not cough it up, my German lines might slip by undetected.

So that is what I did. My eight lines were incorporated into the official German summit translation. With our fingers crossed, we went to the final session of the summit to hear the leaders read their prepared statements and have the lucky simultaneous interpreters in the booths lean back, relax, and just read the written translations, provided the leaders did not deviate from their texts.

Unbeknownst to all of us, the scenario had changed in the last few hours of the summit. Several hijackings of airplanes had happened in the period preceding the summit. One of the worst had been suffered by the German airline Lufthansa in October 1977, a five-day ordeal that took the pirated 737 from Palma to Rome, Cyprus, Beirut, Dubai, and Aden, where the German captain was brutally executed in front of the passengers. The first officer was then forced to fly the plane to Mogadishu, the capital of Somalia. There, a German commando unit rushed in and managed to surprise the terrorists and kill three of the four on board, finally rescuing the passengers.

The hosting Germans spent the last remaining time of the summit persuading the other leaders to agree to issue a joint "Statement on Airhijacking," which invoked sanctions against all countries refusing extradition or prosecution of hijackers. Several American planes had also been hijacked and forced to fly to Cuba. When that joint statement was finally hammered out, there was no more time for the carefully crafted concluding statements by the leaders. Our translations were no longer needed.

A few weeks later, Heinz Weber got in touch with me. They had located the poem in German. It was indeed *"Die Horen."* By dint of luck and poet's intuition, my Bonn translation of the eight lines matched Schiller's original, except for three words, with all the original rhymes in place.

WILLIAMSBURG 1983

In 1983, two years after Ottawa, it was Ronald Reagan's turn to host the Ninth Economic Summit. The restored colonial town of Williamsburg in Virginia was chosen for the event. The principals were to hold their meetings at the Governor's House. At that time, Nora Lejins was the chief of Language Services at the State Department and responsible for organizing the language support. She had sent our chief interpreter, Donald Barnes, to Williamsburg to arrange for lodging, office space, transportation, and the installation of interpreting booths for our large language team.

The White House on-site coordinator had not been to an economic summit before and had no idea of the importance of the language component for the smooth functioning of the event. Interpreters and translators were at the bottom of his priority list. Barnes came back and dejectedly reported to Lejins that the linguists had been assigned the least desirable hotel space, insufficient means of transportation between the various sites, interpreting booths in rooms without air conditioning, and worst of all, office space in a condemned building with dirty and nonfunctioning restrooms.

Lejins, a naturalized immigrant from Cologne, Germany, was furious and called me to her office. She ordered me to arrange a follow-on meeting with the site coordinator in Williamsburg. She said something like this: "Maybe I need to send a Prussian down there to talk turkey to this man. Tell him that I will not agree to any of his arrangements. I will not provide language support under those conditions. Please go down there and throw the book at him. Do not capitulate under any conditions. Be tough as nails."

It was the first time that Language Services was sending me on a management mission rather than an interpreting assignment. As a veteran White House interpreter, I knew well how difficult this would be. The other man held all the cards. His interests were totally different from ours. I made dozens of telephone calls, trying to no avail to get an appointment with him. He was too busy with more important matters. Finally, one late afternoon, I got an appointment for 10:00 pm, barely enough time to drive down there. I jumped in my car and zipped down I-95. Near Richmond, I was pulled over by the Virginia State Police for speeding but was able to talk the trooper out of a ticket and went on with just a stern warning.

At 10:30, I walked into our assigned office space; the dilapidated building was a house of horrors. It had no electricity, so we inspected everything with flashlights. The stench in the restrooms was suffocating. I was told not to worry. Things would be fixed up. As we left the building, I threw down the gauntlet as instructed. "The interpreters and translators will walk into this building over my dead body," I said verbatim. "If you do not wish to change the arrangements completely, you may tell the White House that the Department of State will be unable to furnish any interpreting and translating for this meeting."

The hammer blow worked wonders. We retreated to his office, where he laid the blueprints of all available buildings before me. All office space had been given away. I pointed to a small block of assigned hotel rooms near the principal sites and told him that they could easily be converted into office space. The few guests could be lodged a little farther away. The parking space in front of those rooms could be used for two minibuses to transport interpreters to the various sites. To my amazement, he agreed. By midnight, most of our needs had been agreed to. Maybe without knowing it, the White House coordinator had just made a major contribution to the success of the summit.

The Williamsburg Summit was held in late May but the weather was hot and humid. I worked mostly as a bilateral interpreter, shadowing German Chancellor Helmut Kohl, who was accompanied by his vice chancellor and foreign minister, Hans-Dietrich Genscher.

In his early years as chancellor, Kohl was very difficult to interpret into English. His German sentences tended to be long, with clauses strung together in such a confusing jumble that he occasionally could not track them himself anymore and would forget to insert the verb at the end. He knew only a few words of English, but had studied French and Latin. As a history major, he liked to reference ancient battles and events as well as quote phrases in Latin or French. The problem with his French and Latin was that he pronounced them with such a strong German accent that we interpreters mistook them for German words that we somehow just could not identify.

Kohl also liked simple folksy expressions and would say things like, "*Wir müssen von einem Nebeneinander zu einem Zueinander und dann zu einem Miteinander und Füreinander finden.*" Literally translated, "We must get from an alongside-each-other via a towards-each-other to a with-each-other and for-each-other." Sentences like this would panic most interpreters. Only a few veteran cool cats could turn this into, "We must find our way from parallel actions to mutual approaches and from there to joint actions and complete cooperation." That is what he meant, he just did not say it very elegantly.

Fortunately for me, I had known Kohl since I first interpreted for him at Georgetown University in 1966. By the time he became federal chancellor in 1982, I had already become pretty adept at deciphering his amorphous language, compounded by occasional mumbling. As I had gone to college in his home state of Rhineland-Palatinate, where he had been governor, I was used to the Palatinate style of diction and was familiar with the local wine and food terminology. All of that came in handy during his sixteen years as chancellor.

Similarly, I had gotten to know Genscher quite well. Both of us had escaped from Communist East Germany to the free part of Germany. I admired his astonishing skills as foreign minister and statesman and his deep grasp of the German language. He, in turn, liked the way I handled German and was constantly improving his English by listening to Heinz Weber and me during interpretations. At the beginning of the Carter administration, when I arrived in Bonn one morning after an overnight flight from Washington with newly appointed Secretary of State Cyrus Vance, Genscher was there to greet Vance in front of the television cameras. Tired and bleary-eyed, I whispered Genscher's welcoming remarks to Vance. Then the secretary stepped up to the microphones to make his arrival statement. I whipped out my notepad, ready to take my consecutive notes. Before Vance could utter a word, Genscher said to him in English, into the open mikes, "Your interpreter speaks better German than I." This was a nice compliment from a man who has enriched the German political vocabulary with such clever terms as *Nachrüstung* (a one-word gem that implied that the Soviets had deployed missiles first, and the West was just following up).

So, one day, at the Williamsburg Economic Summit, we had a cocktail reception on the lawn in front of the building where lunch was being prepared. President Reagan was chatting with Kohl, Genscher, Margaret Thatcher, Prime Minister Yasuhiro Nakasone, and others. When it was time to go in for the lunch, a presidential aide came running out of the building and whispered to Reagan, "We had a fire in the kitchen. Lunch will be delayed at least fifteen minutes."

Needing to entertain his guests a little longer, the president dipped into his endless repertoire of jokes, surrounded by more than a dozen foreign dignitaries and three interpreters. I started to interpret the first joke into Kohl's ear, but he waved me off: "I have heard that one before." When it turned out that he had also heard the second joke before, he took me by the arm and said, "Herr Obst, let's take a little walk around the garden." Genscher saw his chance to get away and joined us. So there I was, walking around the garden with Kohl on my left and Genscher on my right, making small talk in German and sharing some laughter. When we passed by the building, two suspicious White House aides stood on the steps, and we overheard one asking the other, "Are you sure that is *our* interpreter?"

At that time, in the Soviet Union or in East Germany, suspicion cast on an interpreter by an influential aide might cost a career or even a life. French, German, and Italian leaders usually treated their interpreters with the same respect as their close aides. They liked to see them seated during meals and would not hesitate to strike up a private conversation.

When I arrived at the chancellery in Bonn one day, one minute ahead of the limousine carrying Vice President Bush, Helmut Kohl grabbed my hand as I was getting out of my embassy car and inquired in front of the television cameras how my mother was doing (she lived in the nearby city of Essen). I felt a little uncomfortable, but European diplomatic interpreters would not have given it a second thought. They expect to be treated like friends.

In grim contrast to this, when I was interpreting for a week in Communist East Germany, an East German interpreter asked me a private question during an evening reception. The very young woman wanted to know whether the racial tensions between blacks and whites were as bad in the United States as she had been told. I answered the question as honestly as I could, neither belittling nor exaggerating the problem. The next morning, she did not return and was replaced by another interpreter.

How close some European leaders feel to their interpreters was also illustrated at the 1983 Williamsburg Summit. During a refreshment break at a chiefs-of-government session, French President Francois Mitterrand wanted to have a chat with Prime Minister Thatcher. An interpreter came over to help, but Mitterrand would not use him and called out loudly for Christopher Thiery. He actually kept Thatcher waiting until Thiery arrived from another room, an astonishing act by a Frenchman toward a distinguished lady. A similar situation played out twice at the Houston Economic Summit. Again, Mitterrand would only speak through Christopher Thiery.

LONDON 1984

In my entire career, I never encountered a better English-German diplomatic interpreter than Heinz Weber. But even Weber occasionally had trouble interpreting Kohl into English. At the London Summit in 1984, President Reagan had invited the chancellor and Foreign Minister Genscher to a bilateral meeting. Edwin Meese and George Shultz were in the meeting room with the president.

When the German party arrived, Heinz rushed over to me and suggested that I should do Kohl into English and he would work into German. This took me completely by surprise. "But Heinz," I said, "We cannot do this. I have not read your delegation's briefing book and you have not read ours."

"We do not need the briefing books to do this right. You usually can do Kohl better than I." Before I could say more, the handshakes were over and Reagan started to speak substantively. Heinz immediately interpreted him into German, leaving me no choice but to put Kohl into English. Fortunately, no surprise subjects surfaced, and I was able to hold my own.

This turned out to be a blessing in disguise. When the meeting was over, Meese and Shultz praised my interpreting, something they had never done before. They usually heard me interpret into German, so they could not be sure whether I was keeping track or not. When all of the English made sense to them, they felt sure that I had done a good job.

TOKYO 1986

Although I had crossed the Atlantic more than a hundred times, the 1986 Economic Summit in Tokyo brought me across the Pacific for the first time. As I had never been to Japan, I thought it wise to fly two days ahead of President Reagan to get myself adjusted to the new environment and to a jet lag almost double the six-hour transatlantic average. I neither speak nor read Japanese, and at Narita Airport, I was staring helplessly at the many signs in Japanese designating the customs lines one had to walk through. Finally, I spotted a sign in English that read "Aliens." This seemed very appropriate to me, because I felt that I had just landed on another planet. Subsequent events were to confirm that feeling.

Once outside the terminal, things got a little easier. I found somebody who spoke English and guided me to a bus that would stop at the Okura Hotel, where the American delegation was staying for the summit. The bus was to stop at three other hotels first. I was pleased to find out that the bus driver ran a tape in four languages that announced over the loudspeaker when we were approaching one of the hotels and gave other useful information.

Always a curious person, I peered out the window intently and carefully studied everything that appeared before my eyes as we entered the downtown area of gigantic Tokyo. The bus stopped at one of the hotels at precisely 4:00 pm. Across the street from the hotel were two tall skyscrapers, filled with offices. Hundreds of office workers, most of them men, were streaming out of the buildings after the day's work. To my amazement, all of them wore similar dark suits and ties, carried the same type of briefcase, walked in the same stiff but hurried manner, and exhibited the unemotional facial expression of professional poker players. They looked like so many black ants pouring out of an anthill. As they were approaching the bus, a chill ran down my spine. I *must* be on another planet. These could not be human beings. They had to be androids. How could we possibly compete with workers like that? I had only seen such scenes in science fiction movies.

This moment will stick with me for as long as I live. What a quantum leap from the diversity of American society in the 1980s to the stoic homogeneity of the Japanese. This one snapshot spoke volumes.

My next culture shock was coming soon as I arrived at the Okura Hotel, not far from the American embassy. The hotel was empty, awaiting the arrival of the American delegation to the summit. I was one of the first arrivals. Japanese security had formed a tight ring around the hotel. My diplomatic passport was studied carefully and the photo compared with my face two or three times. Then I was allowed to enter. I carried a black travel bag over my shoulder and rolled my suitcase into the lobby. To my astonishment, there was a receiving line of six or seven people lined up ready to greet me. Two bellboys grabbed my luggage, and I started to follow them toward the reception desk. The greeting committee, highest-ranking first and lowest-ranking last, included two managers in dark suits and even a chambermaid in full attire. As I drew even with them in the spacious lobby, they all bowed to me.

I was not ready for this. My grandfather had taught me that Prussians only bow to their king and their flag, and not even to foreign kings. Bowing was not in my nature. But I was now in Japan and an American diplomat. So I stopped, turned toward the receiving line, and bowed my head ever so slightly. This produced a surprising reaction in the Japanese. They all bowed again, much deeper than before, their heads coming down to their knees. I felt more embarrassed than honored.

Two hours later, I was at the American embassy, reporting my arrival and looking for summit documents. When I told them about my experience at the hotel, they asked me to show how I had bowed and broke out laughing. A slight bow like that, I was told, is only reserved for prime ministers and other exalted persons. No wonder the Japanese were shocked and quickly bowed back much deeper. At any rate, I got a better hotel room out of it than I might have gotten had they known that I was just an interpreter.

Two things impressed me in watching television in my hotel room. The Tokyo daily newscasts were available in English through simultaneous translation with the touch of a button. At the end of the report, the two newscasters, a man and a woman, would bow to the audience from their sitting position so low that their noses were touching the desktop. Once or twice each day, English lessons were broadcast on one of the main channels. The conversational instruction was excellent. French and German lessons were available occasionally. This is how a nation builds opportunities for export business. We still do not comprehend the importance of the mastery of foreign languages as a key for opening foreign markets. As a result of this and our enormous federal budget deficits, we constantly run the world's biggest trade deficits, the dollar weakens consistently, and it may eventually disappear as a world currency.

Having little interpreting to do in Tokyo, I was able to walk the streets and parks and stop at a couple of Buddhist temples. For a city of millions, I was surprised at the universal cleanliness. The women, especially, were attractively attired, their faces and hair neatly arranged. Though they were clearly still second-class citizens in 1986, they smiled a lot. The young girls were prone to giggle and chat animatedly as they walked down the big boulevards. By contrast, most men seemed to be all business. Prices in Tokyo were mind-boggling. A pound of beef sold for over twenty dollars. I invited another interpreter to a drink at the hotel bar. The tab for the two drinks was 35 dollars.

HOUSTON 1990

The Houston Economic Summit was unique for many reasons. The selection of the steaming city of Houston in July was an endurance test for the participants. This was mostly based on financial considerations. The federal treasury was empty after eight years of huge budget deficits during the Reagan administration. The new president, George Herbert Walker Bush, had many friends in Texas who were willing to underwrite a large chunk of the expenses, as long as it was held in their state. Rice University was selected as the site.

Since 1984, I had been director of the Office of Language Services at the Department of State. This was the first U.S.-hosted summit on my watch, and it was now up to me to arrange the language support for the meetings. Before reporting on the summit itself, let me use the Houston experience to illustrate what is involved in planning and organizing interpretation and translation for this type of event.

The obstacles were considerable. Rice University is sitting in the middle of the city, surrounded by busy roads. Transportation of the interpreters and translators from and to their hotels would not be easy. The location demanded extra high security and access restrictions. From previous experience, I knew that they were likely to become a problem, as many different organizations would be involved in securing the site.

The university had attractive meeting rooms, but they were small and it was next to impossible to install five interpreting booths and a technician's switching station in three of them. A team of about seventy interpreters and translators were needed just from our side, plus the diplomatic interpreters brought along by the chiefs of government. Holding rooms had to be found for all of them, and space was extremely scarce. A translation center with computers, copiers, dictionaries, and communication facilities needed to be established.

As it often happens, the local organizers could understand security, protocol, catering, and carpool needs, but language support was not on their horizon. The deck was stacked against us, but I had two aces in the hole. First, I had attended many summits as a simultaneous or consecutive interpreter before. The things that tended to go wrong were firmly embedded in my memory. Second, I had Stephanie van Reigersberg. In my second year as head of Language Services, I had appointed her as chief of the Interpreting Division. In 1985, LS was

195 years old, but she was the first woman to ever hold that job. It was always wrongly assumed that it took a man to confront the senior White House aides or the secretary of state when they made unreasonable demands for interpretation or translation. I had known Stephie long enough to be sure that she would stand her ground against anybody, even the president himself.

She now had ably served in that job for five years. From her previous interpreting career, she knew hundreds of the best interpreters around the world. More important, she was liked and respected by them. I could delegate chores to her without ever having to worry or to micromanage her. LS had about twenty interpreters on staff and more than fifteen hundred under contract. But she and I knew that there was not enough talent in that pool to provide excellent service for this type of meeting. Additional interpreters would have to be imported from several countries. I let her work on that problem while I took charge of the logistics.

The logistics proved to be a formidable task. I had to make five advance trips to Houston to solve the many problems and get the local organizers sensitized to our needs. Because the summit arrangements were primarily planned by private citizens from Texas with very little knowledge of interpretation and translation needs or how to deal with the federal government, getting our ducks in a row was a painstaking exercise. For each of the more than a dozen summit sites where official events were scheduled, a "site director" had been appointed. Interpreting was involved at every single site. These site directors were mostly young supporters or operatives of the local Republican party establishment, with no experience in organizing such a complex event for world leaders.

Each site director had his or her own office and virtually total power over their given site. They rarely communicated with each other, although most of their offices were in the same building. I had to deal with all of them, and two or three were hard nuts to crack. Like a honeybee, I floated from office to office, pollinating them with the knowledge of what the other site directors were planning and arranging. Involuntarily, I had assumed a role of coordinator in the summit planning that went beyond language needs into transportation, security, meal planning, protocol, and so on.

Interpreting equipment was the biggest problem. The site directors wanted their sites to look beautiful for the photo ops, and the interpreting booths interfered with that. Fortunately, a very experienced and flexible equipment company, Braehler, had won the contract bid for Houston. They were asked to perform miracles, and they practically did. But to make the impossible possible, their representative and I had to get into some nasty confrontations with a couple of site directors. In the end, function and cosmetics somehow got blended into a useful mixture, and the simultaneous interpreters had an appropriate place to work in.

Getting enough good simultaneous interpreters with experience in economics and finance was another problem, especially for Japanese. In 1990, because of a huge demand and short supply of professional talent, these expert linguists were paid $600 to $1,000 a day in Japan, and close to that in the United States. Government regulations prevented me from paying them more than $400 a day. They not only balked at the low pay, but other employers were routinely flying them first class across the ocean, again something that regulations forbade me to do. We needed to bring in at least half a dozen interpreters from Tokyo. To make things worse, the three principals from the new government in Japan were bringing their wives and had requested additional consecutive interpreters.

The summit date was nearing. Stephie and I had not been able to solve this problem. Then I had an idea. I went to the American summit coordinator at the White House and told him that we needed help from the Japanese government to properly serve the Japanese delegation. Could he request someone from the Japanese Foreign Ministry in Tokyo to come to the White House in Washington to meet with him, and have an official from the Japanese embassy here sit in?

After explaining the problem in general terms, he could then just turn the meeting over to me and let me negotiate a solution. I conjectured that sitting inside the White House rather than in my office at the Department of State would make the Japanese more malleable.

The coordinator agreed, the Japanese officials from Tokyo and the embassy came to the White House, and we hammered out a deal in a couple of hours. The Japanese interpreters would fly business class to Washington on our terms and accept our pay of $400 a day and our preset Spartan government per diem, and the rest of their demands were somehow to be accommodated by their own government. I did not know (and did not want to know) how that would be accomplished. From my side, the interpreters for all language combinations and from all countries would be treated the same.

The American government proved to be a much larger obstacle in getting the interpreters to Houston than the Japanese government. We also needed to import a handful of interpreters from Canada, Germany, the United Kingdom, and Switzerland. This required a temporary H-1B working visa, which had to be applied for and paid for by the employer—in this case, my office. Before leaving for an inspection visit to Geneva, where we maintained an office supplying interpreters and translators for the arms control negotiations with the Soviet Union, I asked my deputy director, Mary Bird, to apply for a global visa for each country, as they were all coming to work at the same event, similar to a baseball team or a theater group. Otherwise, we would have to pay the visa fee separately for each individual. As a government contracting officer, I was required to spend taxpayers' money as wisely and sparingly as I could.

The visas had to be issued by the Immigration and Naturalization Service, as it was called in 1990. From long experience, I knew that there was hardly a more uncooperative, arrogant, and dysfunctional agency in the federal government. But here we needed to support an important meeting hosted by our common boss, the president of the United States. Certainly they would gladly help us with that endeavor. We soon found out that they cared about neither our needs nor those of the president.

In Geneva, I got a call from Mary Bird, informing me that the visas would not be granted. We certainly could find people in the United States who could speak foreign languages, the INS argued. When Mary told them that we needed highly skilled interpreters with knowledge of economics, the INS responded that we needed to furnish proof that each of them had at least a master's degree in economics. Most of them had no such degree, of course. Other degrees and doctorates would not count for working at an economic summit, Mary was told. She played her last trump card: "But these interpreters are urgently needed for the president of the United States." That made no difference, was the reply. The president had to obey the INS rules like any other citizen.

When I got back to Washington, I started to negotiate with the director of the Texas region INS office, located somewhere in New England. I, too, got nowhere with him. A team of interpreters was not the same as a theater group, he informed me. If we could not furnish the proof of degrees in economics, we would have to apply for individual visas for each of them and pay the corresponding fees.

We contacted the White House, explained the situation, and asked somebody high up to put the heat to the INS director for contravening the needs of the president. When we inquired again a couple of days later, the INS director grudgingly offered to issue individual visas without the proof of degrees in economics. I asked him how much the total fee was. I would send him a State Department check right away, because we were running out of time. His answer blew me away: The INS would not accept a check from the federal government. I was the employer, and I would have to rush a personal check to his office. "But I am not a private employer," I replied, "I am a federal contracting officer ordering a service from a sister federal agency for supporting the chief officer of the entire executive branch." This argument made no impression on him. Send your own check or no visas.

The total fee was over $1,200. Mary and I each wrote a personal check for over $600 to the INS and rushed it to their office. The visas came, just in the nick of time.

On July 7 and 8, the interpreters arrived in Houston from three continents and many cities. They received several hours of briefings and documents to study. The translators had set up their office, piled up the dictionaries, and tested the computers with software in several languages. We seemed to be ready to go for opening day, July 9.

As I had anticipated access problems to the site for our interpreters and translators, because of the many different law enforcement agencies involved in controlling it, we had chartered two big city buses and had obtained the proper vehicle access credentials, which were displayed on the windshields of the buses. Early morning on the ninth, our language team was loaded on the two buses. The chief interpreter and I, cellphone in hand and our summit credentials hanging around our necks, led the two buses from the hotels to Rice University. A university entrance gate was on the other side of a busy street on which rush-hour traffic was flowing nonstop because there was no traffic light at the intersection. The gate was controlled by Houston city police.

Participants in the 1990 Houston Economic Summit. From left: EU President Jacques Delors, Giulio Andreotti, Helmut Kohl, Francois Mitterand, President Bush, Margaret Thatcher, Brian Mulroney, and Toshiki Taifu. *White House photo*

I stepped off my bus and into the middle of the street, bringing traffic to a stop by raising my hand like a policeman. The two buses then rolled across the street to the gate. The officers said that they were not familiar with the vehicle credentials. Moreover, except for Stephie and me, nobody on the bus had summit badges. I explained that the badges for the others were waiting inside the university at the security office. Could they please contact that office to verify this? They refused to do that and ordered our buses to turn around and leave.

For the next twenty minutes, we were desperately circling the university with our buses, trying to find a way in while trying to reach the chief of summit security on Stephie's cellphone. We were finally directed to a gate where we were allowed to enter, with barely enough time left to get the interpreters credentialed and to their stations. At last, our language team was in place to serve the president and the summit leaders.

For the leaders, Houston was a summit of familiar faces and old friends. For British Prime Minister Margaret Thatcher, this was her eleventh and last summit. At this point, no other chief of government had attended that many. Two other familiar faces, Francois Mitterrand and Helmut Kohl, coming for the tenth and eighth time, respectively, would hang around for a few more years after John Major replaced Thatcher as prime minister. Brian Mulroney had attended five previous summits for Canada. So, this was a chummy club of old friends, who were also very familiar with the host, because Bush had been vice president for eight years under Ronald Reagan. Except for Mitterrand, they represented the conservative election results of the 1980s. The newcomer among this old guard was Prime Minister Toshiki Kaifu of Japan, while Italian Prime Minister Giulio Andreotti was celebrating a comeback after a ten-year absence.

A frequent subject of the public and private discussions among the old-timers was Mikhail Gorbachev. Most of them had met him by now and were impressed by him, especially Margaret Thatcher. Could the end of the Soviet empire and the cold war be just around the corner? Nobody was more hopeful than Kohl. Such a development might just open a window to German reunification. In 1990, he could not possibly have assumed that this could actually happen on his watch, as it later did.

I knew from many interpreting missions that the British had always been cool to German reunification, and that the French were strongly opposed to it. In 2003, former President G.H.W. Bush recounted a conversation on this subject with a French president in which he was told, "I love Germany. I love Germany so much that I prefer to have two of them." The United States, however, had nothing to fear from a united Germany. Many Americans saw postwar Germany as a more reliable ally and friend than France. Thus, German reunification could only be quickly accomplished by agreement among the United States, Russia, and Germany. And that was the way it later happened.

Gorbachev had sent a message to the summit leaders, outlining his economic plans under perestroika. This overshadowed all other summit discussions. As the economy of most of the attending nations was in good shape, the final communiqué of the Houston Summit dealt more with the Soviet Union, Poland, and Hungary than with the United States, Germany, and Japan.

President Bush was a gracious and relaxed host. Saddam Hussein's invasion of Kuwait was still a month away. Despite the excitement over perestroika, the summit atmosphere was easygoing and hopeful. The president called Kohl by his first name and vice versa. Having enough interpreters around the table for the dinners, with the leaders' wives also in attendance, was a tough problem for the chief interpreter and the protocol people to solve. English, German, French, Italian, and Japanese were swirling around the room, and many language bridges were needed. A few strategically placed interpreters would sit on small chairs behind the principals. A few reserves were held just outside the room and would slip inside as needed, often just standing, bent over, between two conversing diners, leaving the room again when no longer needed. There was just not enough space to seat everybody, let alone around the tables. In such a scenario, interpreters do not get to eat and drink, with their favorite wines passing in front of their noses. Most of the interpreters were women. Some of them had to change into evening dresses after the business sessions, fix their hair and faces for a formal dinner, just to stand outside a door on the off chance that they might be needed inside for a few minutes. Those are the moments when interpreters do not particularly enjoy their job and go to bed somewhat frustrated.

Except for a couple of minor equipment failures, the interpretation and translation at all summit events went seamlessly, to everybody's satisfaction. The intensive advance work had paid off. All of us helpers were delighted during the wheels-up party, once the leaders' jets had left Houston.

A few weeks later, the telephone rang at my office in Washington. It was John Condayan, then in charge of administration at our embassy in London. This was the very person who had appointed me head of Language Services in 1984, though I had appeared at the bottom of the list of candidates presented him by the Office of Personnel. He told me that Margaret Thatcher had spoken to her Houston Summit coordinator on her return trip to London and asked him to find out who organized the language support in Houston, because she thought it had worked very well. It was the United Kingdom's turn to host the summit in 1991. She requested that the organizer be brought to London to consult with the Foreign Office on setting up the language support for the next summit.

"Harry," Condayan said, "this is quite a feather in your cap. I do not recall the British ever asking us for advice before."

As a federal employee, I was not allowed to accept money or air transportation from a foreign government, so the State Department paid for my trip to London. When the 1991 Summit at Lancaster House in London was over, the Foreign Office called the embassy again (the summit had been hosted by John Major, since Thatcher had lost the support of her own party and resigned in November 1990). Could Mr. Obst come back to London to be debriefed on how the interpretation and translation had gone? So I made another trip to London, where the British did all the talking, and I could just sit back and listen. This pleased me very much because London had always been my favorite big city in Europe.

PRESIDENTIAL VIGNETTES

JIMMY CARTER

1977–1981

GOOD INTENTIONS AND BAD SURPRISES

To make Washington atone for the sins of Watergate and the arrogance of the Nixon oligarchy, the American voters sent a lay preacher from the Bible Belt to the White House, a serious, introspective, and incorruptible governor from Georgia, speaking softly and flashing a big smile. Carter was also the unmistakable signal that the newly found economic power and huge population increase of the New South could hold its own politically against the already established state powerhouses of the West and the Southwest. Watch out California and Texas! We, too, have money and many electoral votes. Carter was the short Southern overture to the long Clinton opera that was to begin in 1993.

The first time I met Carter was when he paid a visit to the Department of State shortly after his inauguration. I was among a few hundred employees assembled in the Diplomatic Lobby to meet our new president. He gave a brief speech, smiling almost continuously, when his eyes caught a young couple, standing about fifteen feet to his left, holding hands, the way young lovers do. Spotting no wedding rings on their hands, Carter stopped in the middle of his remarks, turned to them, and said, "You two should get married!" The implication seemed to be, "Please, do not live in sin!" Many of us were habitual political analysts. The immediate question popping into our heads was, "Can this Baptist lay minister reinvent himself as the leader of the nation or will it be impossible for him to jump out of his old skin?" We learned later that change did not come easy to Jimmy Carter.

A BAD SURPRISE IN WARSAW

After Christmas 1977, Jimmy Carter set out on an ambitious trip to Europe, India, and the Middle East. The first stop was Warsaw, where he wanted to speak out on peace and human rights under the umbrella of the Helsinki Final Act. President Ford had been in Poland in July 1975, the very day before going to Finland to sign the act. Carter was now in a position to test whether a Communist country would let its citizens listen to such admonitions from a representative of the free world.

The State Department did not have an interpreter on staff who was conversant with the Communist jargon of 1977 Poland. The chief interpreter dipped into his reservoir of hundreds of contract interpreters and selected a gentleman named Steven Seymour. Seymour had mostly worked between Russian and English, but he was born in Poland and had attended Warsaw University. He also had recently interpreted in Polish for a cabinet member and gotten good marks for his work. Therefore, he seemed a good choice for the mission, though he had no experience working at the presidential level.

For an interpreter, traveling with the president can often be living hell, as Seymour was about to find out.

On December 29, Carter was to arrive at a Polish military airfield. The weather was awful: freezing rain with the temperature hovering around 32 degrees F. An extensive advance party from the White House, including a Secret Service detachment, was on the scene, often at loggerheads with Polish security personnel. Seymour had gone to Warsaw ahead of Carter and was driven out to the airbase with other personnel from the American embassy to arrive there two hours before touchdown of *Air Force One*. This was not smart, because the Americans had to stand for two hours in the freezing rain, together with a sizeable press detachment from Poland, the United States, and other countries. The Poles would not allow them inside the buildings for military security reasons.

As Carter's arrival drew near, some of the press were jockeying for advantageous positions to better see and cover the arrival. Some American officials, I was told by people who were there, moved some Polish press back from their front positions to get some of the American press closer. This went over like a lead balloon, and the Polish press was bent on revenge. Imagine Polish officials pushing the American press to the back at an American airfield.

For all of Carter's impending statements, to be aired on Polish television and radio this day and the next, Polish officials wanted their own interpreters to do as much of the interpreting as possible, because this would allow them to tone down remarks on freedom or human rights or to maybe even drop a sentence or two. If the American interpreter could be made to look unreliable or run into problems, that could only help their cause. In addition, the officials probably had some friends in the Polish press corps.

This fiendish scenario was developing as poor Seymour, soaked with cold rain and his jaws almost frozen shut, was hoping to get a copy of the president's arrival remarks, often faxed to the embassy from Washington (or from the airplane if they were still being worked on in flight). Seymour did not get the text to peruse in advance, another complication added to his woes. Even under more normal conditions, doing a presidential speech for the first time on television induces psychological terror for any interpreter.

When the moment came to interpret, Seymour, a talented interpreter, but half paralyzed by the cold and his apprehensions, did not monitor his Polish renditions as well as he would have under normal circumstances. Having worked mostly into Russian in the preceding years, he used a Russian turn of phrase or two, but employed Polish words

A couple of times, he used the wrong verb form to denote the tense. One such formulation implied that Carter had left the United States for good. Any Pole listening to this might get a chuckle out of this slip of the tongue. Obviously, Carter would go back home after the trip. No damage done to understanding. Another time he used a term about cherishing the Polish people that also has a sexual connotation in Polish. No more than an unwise choice of a word carrying several meanings.

After the speech was over, Seymour went on his way to the next interpreting chore, not knowing that within the hour, he would become the most talked about person in the world for days on end. Polish journalists told the non-Polish-speaking foreign reporters that Seymour had said Carter was lusting after the Polish people and that he had no intention of ever going back to the United States. What a coup for the media instead of reporting on a rainy arrival ceremony. A pious Baptist minister lusting after the Polish people! Who would not want to hear about this? Within minutes, the story traveled from Warsaw around the globe.

Federal employees in the United States can only carry a limited amount of vacation days over from one calendar year to the next. If not used, the leave has to be forfeited. This only hurts those employees who are constantly busy and traveling, like interpreters. December was usually the least busy month at Language Services. Most interpreters were on leave on December 30, 1977. Only the chief interpreter, Donald Barnes, and three or four others, including me, were on duty.

When we got to our offices in the morning, all phone lines were ringing off the hook. Calls came in from as far away as Australia, either wanting confirmation on what had happened in Warsaw or bitterly complaining about what Seymour had done. Hundreds of angry calls came in from the Polish-American communities in Chicago, Los Angeles, and other cities. Those we transferred to the Polish desk officer of the department. Unfortunately, his last name was also Seymour. He suffered untold abuse that day and the day after.

Throughout the day, it remained a leading story on radio and television, and in the printed press. Don Barnes was distraught. He told us that this was the greatest disaster ever to befall our office in history, and it was happening on his watch. I retorted that this might actually be a blessing in disguise. Requests for personnel, funds for training, improved working conditions for interpreters traditionally had been assigned a very low priority in the federal government, including in our own agency. Now we were the focus of everybody's attention. Some of our needs might be met in the next few months.

After the Warsaw audiotapes had been evaluated by experts, it became clear that the Polish journalists had greatly exaggerated the interpreter's mistakes. Many days later, with the event still vividly debated in the American media, several of the major papers in New York, Washington, and other cities wrote editorials that exonerated Seymour to a large extent and had some kind words to say about the difficult task of diplomatic interpreting.

The great irony was that Steven Seymour, busy with interpreting meetings and with writing memoranda in Warsaw, never heard what had happened. After the president had left, he took a commercial plane back to New York City. To his surprise, his parents were waiting at the airport, disconsolate and in tears. He assumed that a close relative had died. It was only then that he learned about the worldwide media circus in which he had been the clown.

President Carter wrote him a kind note, thanking him for his work in Poland. Someone, perhaps an angry White House aide, may have had a hand in making sure that he never got it. Days later, Donald Barnes found out about the missing original and obtained an existing copy of it, which he was able to send to Seymour.

The brouhaha became, indeed, a blessing in disguise for Language Services. We were granted access to the White House speechwriters and their drafts of presidential remarks for the balance of the Carter administration. Some of us were even invited to help with writing those speeches, drawing on our intimate knowledge of the cultures and languages involved. Unfortunately, this came to an end again in 1981 when a new team took over White House operations.

WAS IMMER SEI, BERLIN BLEIBT FREI

In 1978, it was Germany's turn to host the G7 Economic Summit. Chancellor Helmut Schmidt invited Carter to come two days early for a state visit. The president accepted, and the White House speechwriters had a number of speeches to draft, with the keynote address to be given in front of the Berlin Airlift Memorial. Due to the new policy, interpreters could contact the speechwriters, and speechwriters would occasionally call us for advice.

One day, the phone rang at my office. The call came from James Fallows, Carter's chief speechwriter. He told me about the planned keynote speech for Berlin. The president wanted to include a sentence in German, similar to Kennedy's famous line, *"Ich bin ein Berliner!"* Could I come up with a line in German that would make a similar impact?

President Carter greets the three interpreters assigned to his 1978 visit to Germany. From left: Gisela Siebourg, Harry Obst (shaking hand), and Heinz Weber. *White House photo*

I told Fallows that I was doubtful that this could be done. Kennedy's line was delivered at a time in the history of Berlin where his visit and his pronouncement made for a perfect fit. Carter's visit would not have the same impact. Fallows basically agreed with my analysis, but he said, "Listen, Harry, the president wants this done. So you and I better deliver."

For two or three days, I wrestled with this problem. The German language is full of *umlaute*, vowels that do not exist in English. Pronouncing them is no problem for Frenchmen, because they have the same vowels, but they are torture for speakers of English. In addition, the German "ch," a frequently occurring consonant, has different pronunciations, none of which occur in English.

It the president was going to pronounce the line so all Germans could understand it, it should not contain any *umlaute* or any *ch*. Naturally, whenever I came up with a somewhat suitable sentence in my mind, I had to throw it out again because of pronunciation hazards.

Finally, one morning, shaving in front of my bathroom mirror, it came to me: *Was immer sei, Berlin bleibt frei!* Loosely translated, "No matter what may be, Berlin will stay free!" The rhymed sentence had a concise punch and cheerful ring to it and spoke to the fear in each Berliner's heart. Their city was still surrounded by divisions of Soviet and East German soldiers, their freedom constantly in jeopardy.

I called the White House. Fallows liked what he heard. The next day, he called me back again. The fellows at the National Security Council, although agreeing that the sentence was in line with our Berlin policy, were objecting to it. The sentence was "too corny," "not presidential."

"Tell the people at the NSC that they do not understand what kind of language Berliners like," I retorted. "I will bet anyone of them 100 dollars that this sentence will be the headline in half of the Berlin papers the next day. It will go over just fine." Unfortunately, nobody took me up on this bet.

In contrast to the lofty thinkers at the NSC, Jimmy Carter liked the line and decided to end his Berlin speech with it. He sent a small tape recorder to my office at the State Department. I spoke the line onto the tape two or three times, so he could practice it. But before getting to Berlin, we first had to go to Bonn, Wiesbaden, and Frankfurt, with other speeches to be interpreted in each place.

Although I was on board *Air Force One* on the flight to Bonn, Carter never ran his pronunciation by me on the plane. He also had inserted a much more difficult sentence in German from Schiller's "Ode to Joy" in his Bonn speech: *"Alle Menschen werden Brüder, wo dein sanfter Flügel weilt."* We did not practice it together, and it did not sound very good when he delivered it in Bonn.

Wading into a crowd, even a friendly crowd, can be dangerous for visiting dignitaries and for their interpreters. In Bonn, the First Lady decided to leave her limousine and plunge into the crowd to shake a few hands on the square where the president had just spoken. Because this was unscheduled, there were no German police at that immediate spot to protect her, just her Secret Service detail. Once people realized what was going on, there was an enormous rush of people trying to get close to her. I was tagging along with her to interpret when a wave of people was pressing hard toward us from three sides. The Secret Service quickly formed a wedge to get her back to her car, but I got pushed back.

Realizing that I might get trampled to death if I fell, I straddled my legs, crossed my arms in front of my chest to protect my ribs, and struggled to stay on my feet. At a moment like this you are gripped by fear, even if you can keep your composure. Your heart races, your adrenalin surges. Fortunately, I did not fall or get badly bruised and eventually fought my way back to a safe area.

The next day, July 15, challenged the depth of my stamina and resourcefulness. It started with a speech at the Erbenheim Airbase in Wiesbaden, from where we moved by motorcade to Frankfurt. There, Carter was to speak in front of the beautiful city hall. Before we departed Wiesbaden, my German friend and colleague, Heinz Weber, rushed over to my car and handed me two pages of paper he had been given by his chief of protocol. It was the draft of the Frankfurt speech, which the Germans already had but I did not.

The First Family at a reception by the mayor of Bonn. *White House photo*

This gave me a chance to read it through twice before we got to Frankfurt. The speech contained no unexpected surprises or difficult formulations. Little did I know that my interpretation of this speech would come back to haunt me for months. Before it was the president's turn, I whispered the German speeches to Carter, who was sitting on my left, while Heinz, sitting between Rosalynn Carter and Secretary Vance, was whispering his own translation to both of them. Then, the president and I rose for his address. At one point, Carter inserted a sentence that had not been in the draft: "We pray that Germany will be reunited one day, because that would be the expression of the will of the German people."

In that period, whenever the subject of German reunification came up, a loud alarm bell would go off in the interpreter's head. We were for it, but the British, the French, and the Soviets were against it, the Russians openly, the French and the British tacitly. Any statement on the subject was like a stick of dynamite and had to be handled with care.

I quickly analyzed the sentence. The only problem was how to translate the word *pray*. In the Bible Belt, where Carter had grown up, the word often just means *hope*, like in "We pray that it won't rain for the picnic on Sunday."

Carter had made a statement on reunification in Bonn, the day before, in which he had actually used the verb *hope*. Another reason to stick with "*hoffen*" in German rather than with "*beten*" (pray) was that this was Carter's first visit to Germany. When Foreign Minister Genscher had returned from Washington after his first meeting with Carter, he had described him as "*ein religiöser Schwärmer*." That term is open to many interpretations, from "a religious dreamer" to "a religious zealot." This comment was still reverberating in the German media. Using "*beten*" would have added fuel to this fire, giving many Germans too one-dimensional a picture of our president.

The above description of my quick analysis gives the reader a good example of how many things an interpreter has to consider within seconds if he wants to come up with the best translation that fits the context and the moment. So, I used "*hoffen*," feeling reasonably sure that this was what Carter meant.

From Frankfurt, we flew to Berlin across the ugliest border anywhere in the world. East and West Germany were divided by a razed gray and brown strip, almost a mile wide, filled with barbed wire, walls, mines, fences, watchtowers, booby traps, searchlights, and shepherd dogs. Like an enormous gaping wound, it stretched for hundreds of miles from the Baltic Sea to the Czech border. No trees, no bushes, no place for a mouse to hide. Formerly busy roads, canals, and railroad tracks were severed by it, making all of Communist East Germany one gigantic prison. Having to fly at the imposed restricted altitude of 10,000 feet made it all the more visible, and on descent into the free part of the city, the Berlin Wall appeared below, separating truth from lies, and relatives from the rest of their city brothers and sisters. This flight reminded all of us why the Berlin Airlift had been necessary and why Carter had come to commemorate it thirty years later with his speech.

From Tempelhof Airport, we made our way directly to the Airlift Memorial Square, jammed with Berliners looking up at the elevated platform for the dignitaries. Carter's speaker's podium had been flown in from Washington for the occasion. Once again, separate microphones for my translation of the speech were about forty feet to the left to keep me out of the television picture, even though there were two dozen other people to Carter's immediate left and right, including Chancellor

Schmidt's interpreter. Clearly this was the work of the White House advance party. The Germans would never have come up with such an idea.

In possession of the draft of this speech for days, I had prepared a written translation into German on four letter-size pages. This was going to be easy. Berlin was sunny but very windy that day. When Carter rose for his speech, I left my notepad in my jacket pocket and pulled out the four pages and a pen, in case he made any changes or additions. The wind was tearing at my pages. I held onto them tightly. The president was to speak in two or three-sentence segments, then pause each time for the translation.

I turned my head to Carter; he was looking at me and saying something that I could not hear, being too far away and because of the noise made by the strong wind. He cupped his hands around his mouth and shouted, "I am going to do it all in one piece." This I heard, but it made no sense. In front of me were microphones connected to German-language television and radio networks in Germany, Austria, and Switzerland. The speech was fourteen minutes long. At least half of the Berliners in front of him did not understand enough English and also would have to wait that long before knowing what he was saying to them. It would also cut down on the applause. Being separated from him, I could not talk him out of it.

Helmut Schmidt speaks to the press in the Bonn Chancellery.
President Carter listens to his interpreter. *White House photo*

That was my first surprise. A few sentences into his speech came the second one. Somebody had handed him a list of war veterans who had flown planes into Berlin during the airlift and had been invited to attend this commemoration. He acknowledged their presence and began to read their names. I furiously tried to write them into the first of my four pages, but I could only understand half of them, in the howling wind and being too far away. Nor was I totally sure about the names I was writing down from the phonetic snatches that reached my ear. Had I been next to him, I could have used the same list for my translation.

At the end of his speech, he delivered *"Was immer sei, Berlin bleibt frei!"* flawlessly and was rewarded with thunderous applause. When the applause died down and he nodded to me for the interpretation, the advance party's strategy of keeping me out of the television picture backfired badly. All the TV cameras swung over to me, and I was on German television almost continuously for fourteen minutes, having to do the entire speech from beginning to end. Nobody was more delighted about this than my mother, who was watching in Essen, Germany, where she lived. She had always complained that I was only shown for a few seconds whenever I came to Europe to interpret. "They finally did it right," she told me in a telephone call two days later. I was not pleased with my performance, because I was forced to leave out the names of the airlift pilots, and I felt bad about it. When I, too, ended with, "*Was immer sei …,*" another wave of frenetic applause swept over the square. The next day, the phrase was the headline in all the major Berlin papers and in more than half of all other German newspapers. It did not match Kennedy, but it made an impact.

There was no time to bask in my brief moment of glory. I had to rush to the Kongresshalle, where Carter was going to hold a long town meeting with Berliners and have a question-and-answer session with them. I hustled up unfamiliar stairs, found the interpreting booths, briefly greeted my German colleagues who were providing the German-to-English translation, put on my headphones, and had to switch my brain to simultaneous interpreting, after having worked the trip in consecutive up to this point.

I stumbled a couple of times in the first phrases before warming to the task. I still remember my surprise when the president was asked how much allowance he was giving his daughter Amy, who was along for the trip. The answer was, "Zero." I wondered whether I was too generous with my own daughters.

The town meeting, also carried live on television and radio, was warmly received by the people of all ages and backgrounds who were in attendance. The president, his family, and his aides were delighted. This was probably the most successful and enjoyable day Carter ever had on a foreign trip. Everybody was in a good mood when we made our way back to Bonn for the G7 Economic Summit, which was to begin next morning and is described in another chapter.

ONE WORD OUT OF THOUSANDS

In Bonn, I stayed at the Steigenberger Hotel, which was conveniently located near the chancellery and the Foreign Office. The German Office of Language Services (*Sprachendienst*) occupied a beautiful mansion behind the new modernistic chancellery.

Early on Monday, July 17, the last day of the G7 Summit, I had just returned to my room from breakfast when the phone rang. It was Heinz Weber, the German chief interpreter. Had I read *Die Welt* that morning? *Die Welt* is a large-circulation national daily, read all over Germany. I had not. Heinz asked me to come over to his office right away.

When I got there, he closed the door and handed me the paper. He pointed to an article, written by Diethart Goos, entitled "Interpreter weakens passage on reunification." It was about the sentence in the Frankfurt speech, "We pray that Germany will be reunited one day, because that would be the expression of the will of the German people." In the article I was called an "imprecise interpreter" who had supplanted the word *hope* when *pray* was clearly what the president had said and meant. He even contended that the German equivalent "*wir beten*" was not strong enough, I should have said, "*wir beten zu Gott*" ("we pray to God").

Heinz told me that my translation was utterly defensible, given the context in which the word *pray* appeared. He also told me to expect a lot of trouble as a result of this article, and was he ever right. For weeks, letters from outraged Germans arrived at the White House, the Department of State, and our embassy in Bad Godesberg. The embassy had to deal with this issue in a news conference. Heinz defended me in a newspaper interview on the same subject.

Back in Washington, reading many of those letters, I decided not to respond. I knew I had used sound judgment in translating that sentence. It was just one word of the many thousands I had put into German during the president's trip. Even if I had been dead wrong, that would still be a pretty good batting average. I was not about to pour my own fuel on the spreading fire.

However, a few weeks later, I made one exception. A German lady named Ilse Henkes, who had lived and worked in the United States for fourteen years, wrote that the Americans were a praying people in contrast to the Germans. For that reason alone, I should have used *pray*. I obviously did not believe in prayer or I could not have made such a mistake. She seemed to be a sweet person whom I had offended. I sent her a letter, explaining, step by step, how I had come up with my decision. She sent me a nice response, stating that she did not know that interpreting was that difficult. Maybe I had done the right thing after all. Later she sent me a Christmas card.

TO VIENNA WITH GOOD INTENTIONS

Eleven months after the Germany trip, I was on *Air Force One* with President Carter again, this time to another German-speaking nation,

Austria. At that time, Austria was still a neutral country, making it a good place to meet with our adversary, the Soviet Union. We were going there to sign the SALT II Treaty on strategic missile reductions, even though there was considerable opposition to this agreement in the Senate. Talks on a possible SALT III agreement and other topics were to be held with the ailing Soviet General Secretary Leonid Brezhnev.

When I got on the plane at Andrews Air Force Base, I was happy to see it was the SAM 2700, commissioned by Nixon, rather than the presidential plane with the tail number 2600, which I had usually been on. The 2700 was more comfortable all around, also for those of us who did not rate the better seats. It was June 14, 1979, and my fifty-second Atlantic crossing. To my surprise, I did not get a regular seat, but was put in the forward office cabin in a typing seat, facing sideways, looking at an IBM Electric and a wall without windows. To my right was a table with four seats. Around it sat the four presidential assistants I was by now reasonably familiar with: Hamilton Jordan, Jody Powell, Gerald Rafshoon, and Phil Wise. These were the trusted lieutenants of Carter from his days as governor of Georgia. A small distance beyond the table was the presidential cabin, a small suite of rooms behind a closed door.

After a while, Carter's aides were pouring over several folders containing papers that the president had to make decisions on, some very mundane, some more complicated and weighty. They would discuss those issues, come to a consensus, and write a recommendation for the president on what to do. This was probably what they did at the White House every day. I was now the fly on the wall, listening to those discussions while pinned to my uncomfortable seat for the eight-hour flight.

This flight confirmed to me what some of us at the Department of State had considered a mistake made by the president after his election. Being a good, kind, and loyal person, he had taken his Georgia aides with him to Washington and put them into important positions. All of them were young, bright, and action-oriented, but almost totally lacking in national and international experience. They were probably one of the reasons that the Carter administration did not accomplish more than it did. With fifteen years of Washington government experience under my belt in 1979, I was astonished and disappointed to hear some of the arguments they made and the recommendations they ended up with. By now, they had been in Washington almost four years and should have come up with more promising conclusions. When some good arguments were put forward, they most often came from Hamilton Jordan. The president was known to be a micromanager at heart. I felt sure he would not adopt some of that day's recommendations after thinking them through.

At one point, the First Lady and young Amy Carter came into the office cabin. Amy was holding a violin and began to play some practice passages on it. When I was young, I had studied the violin for a couple of years and had developed a good ear for the right and the wrong notes. This little practice session was quite a torture for my ears. Amy was obviously a rank beginner, though playing with bravado. When she hit a couple of right notes, it was probably by accident, because they were few and far between. Of course, nobody said anything critical. Her mother praised her for her effort. Some of us were greatly relieved when Amy put the instrument away and started doodling on a piece of paper instead.

About two hours out of Vienna, the Georgia Foursome was discussing the draft of Carter's arrival remarks at Schwechat Airport. We were to be greeted by President Rudolf Kirchschläger and Chancellor Kreisky. Brezhnev was scheduled to arrive many hours after us. When they were finished, Rafshoon handed me the text, so I could familiarize myself with it for my interpretation into German. The text dealt mainly with the Soviets and arms reduction issues. There were no acknowledgments at the beginning. I walked over to Rafshoon, as communications were his responsibility, and said, "We need to start with 'Mr. President, Mr. Chancellor' at the minimum. Do you think we should recognize anybody else, like our ambassador?"

"There will be no acknowledgments," Rafshoon responded. "We are not going to Vienna to meet with the Austrians, we are going there to meet with the Russians."

"But we cannot do that," I protested. "We will be landing on Austrian soil, greeted by the Austrian president, and all of Austria will look in on television. If we do not want to say anything about Austria, at least we will have to acknowledge the presence of the country's two top leaders. The Austrians are a friendly nation. There is such a thing as diplomatic protocol."

Rafshoon gave me a sarcastic smile. Who was I to lecture him? "There will be no acknowledgments, and that is that." Press Secretary Jody Powell agreed with him.

I went back to my seat. This made no sense. The Austrians would be peeved, and rightly so. What possible benefit could our president gain by leaving out the customary acknowledgments? As an interpreter, I had an option here. I could just put in the acknowledgments in my German rendition. If called on it, I could say, "Gosh, I am sorry. I am so used to doing this at airports, I forgot it was not actually said by the president."

After some reflection, I decided against it. If the president was going to leave it out, I would leave it out. Why should I bail out his assistants after they brushed off my arguments like that? On arrival, Carter did not acknowledge anybody, nor did I. Nobody said anything to us in Vienna, but the next day, this diplomatic faux pas drew negative comments in a couple of Austrian newspapers.

A DAY OF UNEXPECTED ADVENTURES

The day after our arrival, Friday, June 15, was supposed to be my easy day in Vienna. Except for a brief late afternoon welcoming meeting with the Austrian president and Chancellor Kreisky, also to be attended by General Secretary Brezhnev, followed by a Mozart opera at the Staatsoper, there was nothing on my agenda.

The opera was going to be black tie. When I took my tuxedo shirt out of my suitcase, I found the collar badly wrinkled, probably the result of the Secret Service's thorough search of everybody's luggage. Getting a collar pressed quickly at a small hotel is easy; at a big city hotel, it requires extensive negotiation with the assistant manager. When it was ready, I went to our embassy with my tuxedo bag over my shoulder, because the interpreters had a holding room there for the entire visit.

This was an important event. In addition to the president, the Secretaries of State and Defense, Cyrus Vance and Harold Brown, and National Security Advisor Zbigniew Brzezinski were in our party and would have occasional talks with their counterparts in the Soviet delegation. We had all of our Washington staff interpreters for Russian in Vienna, and had brought two more in from Geneva, where Language Services maintained a branch office to serve the arms control and disarmament negotiations with the Soviet Union. My Washington staff colleague Gisela Marcuse was also present to help with German interpreting. Chief Interpreter Donald Barnes was along to supervise us and run our temporary field station.

I reported to Don, and greeted my colleagues who had come in on different planes. Next, I went around the embassy to greet some of the personnel I knew from previous visits to Vienna. At about 11:30, I was sitting in the office of the political counselor, Woody Romine, enjoying a cup of coffee and a friendly chat, when somebody rushed in and told me that I needed to get to the residence of Ambassador Wolf immediately. The president was leaving for an unscheduled outing at noon and needed me.

The ambassador's residence was a good distance from the embassy. It took me a few minutes to secure a car from the motor pool and rush off with an Austrian contract driver, who did not understand English. We had to drive through the heart of busy Vienna. On some streets, we were running parallel to streetcar tracks and had to stop for every trolley that was loading and unloading passengers. It was a warm and sunny day. Many old ladies were out for a walk with their dachshunds, crossing slowly in front of us. Vienna does not run at the pace of New York City. The precious remaining minutes were ticking away.

We reached the street where the residence sat on a small hill exactly at noon. As we were trying to make our right turn into it, the road had just been blocked by Austrian police. They signaled for us to drive straight on. Half of the president's motorcade was slowly driving down the street toward us, the other half was still rolling down the hill from the residence into the street. I yelled at the driver in German, "Pull onto the sidewalk!" He said that was *verboten*, but he finally reluctantly complied. By now, the convoy was moving at a faster pace. A black limousine was passing in front of me. I jumped out of my car, opened the door of the limo, and swung myself inside, instantly facing a startled Secret Service agent, who reached for his handgun. Fortunately, he saw the pin on my lapel, identifying me as a member of the presidential delegation, and made no attempt to shoot me. It was the car of the First Lady, who was not in it because she had joined her husband in the lead car.

I fell back into a seat, mopped my brow, and asked the agent where we were going. He answered that the president had decided to go to a monastery restaurant for lunch. Brezhnev's motorcade was moving around downtown Vienna, so we, too, were going to show our flag to the Austrians. We went a good distance to Klosterneuburg. The monastery's Stiftskeller restaurant had an outdoor terrace with a nice view. We gathered around a long table with Carter at the head of it, the First Lady, Amy, and the Vances closest to us. It was a good thing that I had risked the leap into the limousine, because my colleague Gisela Marcuse, having no assigned seat, had missed the motorcade when it suddenly moved down the ambassador's driveway.

Neither of the two waiters serving us spoke English, so I had to read the menu to everybody and place the orders. I pulled up a chair behind the president and, as usual, never got to eat. When it was time for the dessert menu, I read out the options aloud.

Then I asked Mrs. Carter first and Mrs. Vance second what they had chosen and passed this along to our waiter. Next, I turned to the president and asked, "Mr. President, have you made a selection?"

Carter looked at me with a scowl and said with some emphasis, "I made my selection a long time ago."

This flustered me. Was he annoyed at me for asking Mrs. Vance before him or was it just the jet lag we were all suffering from? As an interpreter, you cannot dwell on a mistake or mishap, perceived or real, you have to move on with your work without burdening your soul.

After lunch, we went down long wooden stairs into the monastery's famous wine cellar for a tour. There were several rooms down there, big and small vats, shelves with hundreds of bottles, and a couple of rooms with tables, where the monks may have feasted for a couple of centuries.

The abbot had been away from the monastery when he heard on the news that he had distinguished visitors. He had hurried back to Klosterneuburg, decorated a table in one of the cellar rooms with an American flag, and ordered a couple of bottles of his best champagne to be opened. Then he sent an assistant to the room where we were touring with an invitation to come to that room and drink a toast to peace with him.

The president had just disappeared into the cellar's restroom by himself when this emissary arrived, whose invitation I was interpreting into English for our party. Phil Wise, who accompanied us for the luncheon party, ever the protective appointments secretary, said to me, "Tell him thank you for the invitation, but we are already late and must depart immediately."

Once again, I listened to a presidential aide in disbelief. Another five or ten minutes would not jeopardize our late afternoon appointment at the Hofburg. In my mind, I was visualizing the morning papers: "Carter comes uninvited to monastery. Refuses to drink a toast to peace with the abbot who had rushed back to greet him."

Instead of translating into German to the emissary what I had been told to say, I zipped over to the door of the men's room, where Carter was just emerging, and said to him, "The abbot has just arrived and would like to drink a toast to peace with you." Carter readily agreed and overruled his protesting aide. We walked over to the other room, drank a couple of toasts, and made the entire monastery happy. The next day, the papers gave this little gesture positive coverage.

The cellar tour completed, we made our way up the steep wooden stairs. The president and Cyrus Vance were ascending side by side, talking and not watching their steps. Carter's bodyguard was right behind him while I was following Vance. Suddenly, both men stumbled and lost their balance. I quickly grabbed Vance under his shoulders and steadied him, but the president fell forward, breaking his fall with his hands. Fortunately, he did not injure or bruise himself.

When we reached the top, the Secret Service agent pulled me aside and said, "Next time, get your priorities straight. When the president falls, you do not assist the secretary of state. You help the president." I did not respond to this. I would have been unable to reach the president from my position. However, the bodyguard was directly behind him.

Interpreters do not only serve as scapegoats while they interpret. They sometimes are handy lightning rods.

A few minutes before six in the afternoon, we finally got to see Brezhnev at the Hofburg, the ornate former residence of the Austrian emperors and Empress Maria Theresia. The general secretary, though reportedly ailing, looked well enough and was in a jovial mood. Ten minutes later, all of us joined the Austrian president and Chancellor Kreisky for a photo opportunity, followed by a fifteen-minute courtesy call on the Austrian leaders. As the four principals were standing together and chatting, they were surrounded by four interpreters: Victor Sukhodrev and a German-language interpreter for the Russians, William Krimer and I for the American side. When I saw the June 25 edition of *Newsweek* at Heathrow Airport a few days later, I was surprised to find myself on a magazine cover for the first time, right between Carter and Brezhnev.

KISSING BREZHNEV

After two days of meetings with the Soviet delegation at their embassy and ours, the big event finally took place on June 18: the signing of the second treaty between the United States and the U.S.S.R. on the Limitation of Strategic Offensive Arms (SALT II). I was just a spectator, sitting among journalists in the large Redoutensaal, where William Krimer, our senior diplomatic interpreter for Russian, did a great Russian rendition of Carter's remarks from consecutive notes.

Looking up at the platform where the top dignitaries were seated, I had mixed feelings. I had escaped from the persecution of the East German Communists under a hail of bullets in 1949 and was accused of treason at the age of seventeen. Though all in favor of limiting the large and expensive arsenals of nuclear weapons, I had little hope that the Senate would ever ratify this treaty. My greater worry was that the Soviets saw Carter, who had attended a Catholic mass at the Hofburg the previous morning, as a weak and peace-loving president whom they did not have to fear while pursuing the continued expansion of the Communist quest to conquer the world for their crazy ideology. When Carter embraced and kissed Brezhnev after the signing, I felt a resentful twinge rather than any elation. Six months later, the Soviet tanks rolled into Afghanistan.

Escort Interpreting

Escort interpreters usually accompany foreign visitors during their visits in the interpreter's home country. In a few instances, the interpreter may escort people from his home country into a foreign country. Foreign visitors may be invited under sister cities programs or corporate, athletic, governmental, educational, or research programs.

In the United States, the largest such program is the International Visitor Program. It is a creation of Congress and administered by the Department of State, with the assistance of many private institutions and private volunteers in all fifty states. This hugely successful program has brought many thousands of leaders and potential leaders to the United States for study tours, which often are three to four weeks in length. The "grantees" can come from any area of the foreign society: politicians, educators, artists, engineers, athletes, labor union leaders, agricultural experts, scientists, and so on. They cannot apply for the program but are suggested by Foreign Service officers at the American embassies and missions in other countries. A few who come at their own expense are called "voluntary visitors." They also may receive logistical and programming assistance, and interpreters, if needed.

Hundreds of grantees, invited when they were still potential leaders, later became prime ministers, presidents, or cabinet members in their countries. They will have had a direct and extended look at the American scene and made friends here, remaining in touch with them for many years. Two German chancellors I interpreted for, Willy Brandt and Helmut Schmidt, at times recounted fond or significant memories from their early visits to the United States under this program. The resulting benefit in terms of avoiding conflicts and misunderstandings in the international political and economic arena are substantial and worth many times the cost of the program.

Many grantees do not have sufficient knowledge of English to understand technical briefings or American idiomatic expressions. They are assigned escort interpreters by the Department of State.

TRAVELING THE AMERICAN CIRCUIT: ADVENTURES AND OPPORTUNITIES

The role of the escort interpreter is strenuous but very rewarding. When on the road, there are no eight-hour days. They frequently work twelve to sixteen hours. In addition to interpreting, the interpreter is usually in charge of the daily travel logistics, must keep in touch with the program planners in the next place to be visited, and must make sure the visitors get their daily needs met, be it at a restaurant, bank, post office, dry cleaner, or dentist.

But the most important role of the interpreter is to dispense knowledge about the United States. He is always with the visitors, so he is asked questions first. "How many American workers are in trade unions?" "Do the individual states have the same criminal laws and penalties?" "What is a punt in football?" "What happens at a county fair?" "What is the Electoral College?" "Why do your casinos neither ask for passports nor charge admission?"

The interpreter becomes a professor in a small traveling university. But he also is a student, absorbing enormous amounts of useful information each day. Most visitors and most professional interpreters have university degrees. Issues are probed in depth. A simple answer may not suffice.

As a student, the escort interpreter assigned to the International Visitor Program acquires much new knowledge, some of it of the caliber only found in graduate courses, because many visitors are among the top experts in their field. That is one of the reasons why they were invited. As a result, they are likely to meet with their counterparts here, another exposure to the latest developments in that special field. Over the years, the interpreter travels with experts of many different professions. His general knowledge expands with each trip.

The visitors bring with them the current terminology used in their country. The interpreter gets to update, deepen, and modernize his knowledge of the other language. The translator may not find those expressions in a dictionary until many years later.

And, most useful of all, the interpreter gets to know the United States much better than most other Americans.

When I joined the Department of State in Washington in January 1965 as staff interpreter for German, I was not required to do any escort interpreting. Few staffers ever do. The department has many hundreds of contract interpreters who travel with the foreign visitors.

The chief of the Interpreting Division was surprised when I volunteered to do a couple of trips each year. My rationale was simple. First, as an immigrant who had only been in the country for eight years in 1965, I felt that I had a lot to learn about my adopted country. Second, when you interpret, you cannot look things up in books. You must work with the knowledge stored in your head. For a professional interpreter, no amount of general knowledge is ever enough to accommodate all situations. If I could learn many new things on the road, I was quite willing to put up with workdays that were much longer than at the office in Washington.

During my career, I did twenty-six trips around the United States with foreign visitors. Most were very strenuous, but a few were extremely pleasant. I never regretted one of them. Each time, I came home a better and more knowledgeable person, even in the two or three cases where I despised an obnoxious visitor who had made each day a frustrating chore.

BEARS, RATTLESNAKES, AND BLONDE SCALPS

Almost all German boys born between World War I and World War II read the novels of German writer Karl May. His books were as popular with the young set as Harry Potter books are today. When boy met boy in the United States, the first question often was, "How many baseball cards do you have?" In Germany, the first question was, "How many Karl May books have you read?" About half of his sixty books dealt with American Indians. The Apaches were May's favorite tribe, and the fictional Chief Winnetou was his principal heroic character, possibly inspired by tales about Geronimo. Three of his novels were dedicated to this courageous and noble Indian chief; simply entitled *Winnetou I, Winnetou II,* and *Winnetou III,* they were absolute must reading for all young boys of that time. I still have those books in my private library.

Although May, a high school teacher in Saxony, had not visited North America before writing his exciting Indian stories, he had amassed detailed knowledge about Indian tribes from returning visitors and other sources. He was an avid collector of wampums, tomahawks, moccasins, feathered bonnets, and other Indian gear and artifacts. He knew the Indian customs in war and peace. He knew precisely how they tracked humans and animals, reading the ground like a book.

My first German visitor, a journalist from Recklinghausen, had Karl May firmly embedded in his mind. He wanted to spend much of his study tour out West and in Indian country. Having read a good dozen of May's Indian books myself as a boy made me a suitable escort interpreter.

We toured a good bit of Indian country in Oklahoma, guided by an Indian agent from the Department of the Interior. One day, we visited an elderly Kiowa couple near Apache, Oklahoma. They were farmers owning 320 acres of land. My visitor asked whether the farmer had heard any stories of Indian fights or raids when he was a young boy. The farmer, probably born around 1890, told us about Kiowa and Apache raids into northern Texas, where a number of German farmers had settled and accumulated stores of horses and cattle. He described the painting of the faces, war dances, and other preparations for such raids.

The Indian warriors would usually ride south through the night and raid a farm early in the morning, killing and scalping everybody, including women and children. Afterwards, they would drive the captured horses and other animals back into Oklahoma. "Did they really scalp women and children?" asked my visitor, because the noble Indians in Karl May's stories did not do that. The Kiowa did not answer that question; he rose from his chair, went into another room, opened a closet, and returned with an Indian spear that had about a dozen withered scalps attached to it. Most of them were blonde and some of them looked like they had come from the heads of women and children. A shiver ran down our spine. This kind of history lesson one never forgets.

A day later, we were touring a larger Indian farm. This farmer was young and drove us around his property in a pickup truck. Suddenly, he hit the brakes. On the dirt road, just ahead of us, lay a huge rattlesnake, sunning himself. He said he suspected that this was the large snake that had bitten one of his farmhands in that area a couple of days earlier. He had rushed him to a hospital in Anadarko for antivenom treatment.

We got out of the truck. The farmer bent down and picked up a handful of rocks. He walked right up to the snake, showing absolutely no fear, while we kept a respectful distance. The rattler wound into a tight coil and hissed at him, standing only four feet away. The farmer started throwing rocks at the snake, aiming for his raised head. The fourth or fifth throw found its mark and the snake went limp. The Indian took a spade out of the bed of his truck, severed the rattle from the animal's tail, and handed it to the visitor for a souvenir, still warm and dripping a little blood from the tail. The journalist wanted no part of it. Neither did I. The farmer shook his head; what a bunch of sissies.

After visits to the Grand Canyon and the West Coast, we arrived in Salt Lake City for a look at the Church of Latter Day Saints and visits with Mormon families. This was my first visit to Utah. While I had been reasonably familiar with the terminology of the Indian culture and the names of the tribes, I now found it hard to interpret some of the stories of the Mormon scriptures my visitor was told. There were so many unfamiliar names and places to be dealt with, and there was no logical connection between my conception of history and the Mormon version of it. Once again, I learned how hard interpreting can be in unfamiliar territory.

We toured the Kennecott copper mine near Salt Lake City on Wednesday. Mining downwards in spiraling terraces, the process had created a huge crater so deep that the Empire State Building would submerge in it. The copper is interlaced with gold deposits, making Kennecott also one of the largest gold mines in the United States. We had no appointments scheduled for our last day in Utah, May 27. My visitor suggested that we rent a car and have a picnic at Bear Lake, half in Utah, half in Idaho, on the other side of a 10,000-foot ridge. In late May, it would still be cold at the lake. We bought sandwiches, some fruit, and sodas; threw a couple of sweaters in the backseat; and drove north on Interstate 84 on a beautiful sunny day. There was little traffic on the road. Somewhere north of Brigham City, the few cars ahead of us had come to a stop. A cloud of dust was approaching from the west. Suddenly, we saw cowboys in full gear, lassos tied to their saddles, whips in hand, driving several hundred head of cattle east across the interstate, aided by little dogs with loud barks. My visitor ran forward excitedly with his camera. The Old West was still alive, at least in Utah.

About an hour later, somewhere near Logan, the German spotted a cave in the side of a mountain, just fifty feet or so from the road. Next to the cave, a spring jumped straight out of the rock, creating a tiny waterfall. He asked me to stop the car. By now, his imagination was running away with him. Could Indians have lived in that cave? With a spring right next door, it would have been a perfect dwelling. Could I go and have a look while he watched the car?

Being a naïve rookie escort, I readily agreed and climbed up the gentle slope to the cave. I had no flashlight, but the light of the sun fell into the mouth of the cave. Once I was a few feet inside, there was little light. I stopped to get my eyes adjusted to the dark when my nose picked up a scent. It was an animal scent that I could not identify. A moment later, my eyes noticed a big shadow rising up ahead of me. I turned and ran back out as fast as I could. The moment I reached the car, a big bear emerged into the sunlight, saw that the intruder was gone, and trundled back into the cave.

A short drive later, we crossed over the top of the range and finally could look down on the clear blue-green waters of Bear Lake, at least 2,000 feet below us. It stretches for twenty miles into southeastern Idaho and is about eight miles wide. We enjoyed the breathtaking vista with mountains on all sides. When I serpentined our car down to the shore, I wondered how the pioneer settlers traveling the Oregon Trail had ever managed to get their heavy wagons through these passes, up and down treacherous trails. We talked about that as we had a chilly but happy afternoon picnic by the lake before returning to Salt Lake City.

More stunning vistas lay ahead as we rode the famous *Zephyr* through majestic mountains along the winding railroad tracks from Utah to Denver, where we stayed at the equally famous Brown Palace Hotel, former haunt of the railroad barons. My first escort trip ended here. Another interpreter replaced me, as I was summoned back to Washington to interpret a visit to President Johnson by German Chancellor Ludwig Erhard. I was nervous and not quite ready for such a difficult assignment. Karl May would have correctly called me a mere "greenhorn." I wondered, would I would make it through my baptism of fire without getting scalped?

BECOMING A NUCLEAR EXPERT AND BARELY SURVIVING IT

There is a beauty in discovery. There is mathematics in music, a kinship of science and poetry in the description of nature, and exquisite form in a molecule. Attempts to place different disciplines in different camps are revealed as artificial in the face of the unity of knowledge.

All literate men are sustained by the philosopher, the historian, the political analyst, the economist, the scientist, the poet, the artisan, and the musician.

Glenn T. Seaborg

In November 1970, a group of Austrian nuclear experts were invited to tour nuclear power plants and a uranium processing plant in the United States. The Austrians were about to place an order for nuclear power plants and were close to buying them in Sweden. The Atomic Energy Commission (AEC) in Washington and the Westinghouse Company in Pittsburgh believed that the pressurized water reactor manufactured by Westinghouse was ideally suited for the Austrian needs. Austria had to make a decision on that multimillion-dollar purchase fairly quickly, so time was of the essence. On the request of the Atomic Energy Commission, I became the escort interpreter for this mission.

As a White House interpreter, you meet some of the leading men and women in many fields of knowledge. The president of the United

States usually has access to the best minds. Getting to know and work with some of those personalities is one of the most enjoyable perks of diplomatic interpreting. When I worked for Johnson and Nixon, Glenn T. Seaborg was in Washington as chairman of the Atomic Energy Commission, forerunner of the Nuclear Regulatory Commission. In the 1960s, I had acquired a great personal interest in nuclear physics. I was fascinated by the prospects of fission and fusion and by the healing potential of nuclear isotopes. The AEC published a long series of illustrated paperbacks on nuclear matters that were written in plain language, ideal for people who had no background in engineering and limited knowledge of higher mathematics. I read most, if not all, of them.

The Department of State often received requests for interpreters from other federal agencies. One day, Glenn Seaborg requested an interpreter for German for a discussion of nuclear fuel cycles. I was sent to interpret the meeting and got to meet Seaborg. Looking back over my long career today, I cannot recall anybody who impressed me more. Because the first meeting went well, Seaborg occasionally requested me for other jobs. As a result, I got to know him fairly well. He was unassuming, patient with interpreters, loved to hear and tell a good joke, and had a quick wit, launching some great repartees.

Seaborg was a shining light in chemistry and nuclear physics, particularly transuranium physics. The list of his discoveries and co-discoveries is long, including plutonium, californium, berkelium, curium, americium, seaborgium, and several isotopes for nuclear medicine, such as technicium, iodine-131, and cesium-137. But he was also a profound philosopher, an economist, a political analyst, a fabulous speaker and teacher, and versed in many other areas. Even his commencement speeches at universities were a font of knowledge and wisdom, and showed his keen understanding of the country and world he lived in. He was one of the few of his generation who defended the university students who led protests against the Vietnam War. He understood their feelings. He seemed to understand everything happening on this planet better than most.

Interpreting in physics and chemistry between English and German is more taxing than between English and any of the Romance languages. For the basic substances (oxygen, hydrogen, nitrogen, and so on), the English words have the same Latin roots, making the transfer of terminology easy for the interpreter's mind. Oxygen is *oxygène* in French and *oxígeno* in Spanish, for instance, but the German word is *sauerstoff*, and nitrogen is *stickstoff*. The lack of a common root makes the locating of the terminology in the interpreter's memory banks a trifle more strenuous and time-consuming. In addition, the German words are usually longer and more cumbersome. Seaborg was well aware of this, showed patience, and made the necessary allowances.

The subatomic particles sound a little strange even in English but become outright funny when the interpreter uses his visualization to try and remember them. The basic meaning of *quark* in German is "cottage cheese" when it is not a subatomic particle. By now, years later, we even have up quarks, down quarks, strange quarks, and charmed pentaquarks, making twenty-first-century interpreting in the nuclear world even more difficult to navigate.

My interpreting for the Atomic Energy Commission had now brought me to this Austrian nuclear delegation. The group's itinerary was so crowded that the trip did not fit into commercial airline schedules. After a visit to a uranium processing plant near Columbia, South Carolina, Westinghouse gave the group extensive briefings in Pittsburgh. In both places, my basic knowledge of nuclear matters made interpreting fairly easy. In Pittsburgh, Westinghouse was going to loan us a company plane for the remainder of the trip. We were a traveling party of seven: five Austrians, an expert from the AEC, and me. The weather had turned very ugly when we arrived at the airport. A hailstorm with strong gusts was pelting Pittsburgh when the Westinghouse plane, coming from another city, was landing to pick us up.

The hail hit the nose of the plane so hard that it broke the cockpit windshield. Obviously, we could not use it. There was no commercial flight to Rochester, New York, our next-to-last stop for the day. Westinghouse looked for a charter plane, but nothing big enough for seven passengers could be found. Finally, two small planes were located: a twin-engine Beechcraft-99 that could take four passengers and a single-engine Piper Navajo that three people might get squeezed into. By the time the planes rolled into view, the storm had grown even stronger, the hail mixing with icy rain. Under the conditions, flying aboard the Beechcraft was bad enough, traveling on the Piper struck fear in our hearts.

The Piper had only two seats, one for the pilot, one for a passenger. Behind those seats was a wooden bench that normally held luggage. Two lightweight passengers could be squeezed in there if all the luggage was loaded onto the Beechcraft. Triage had to be performed. James Ammons, the AEC expert, at about 150 pounds, and I, at about 160, were assigned the bench on the Piper. The oldest Austrian, probably an octogenarian, was assigned the front seat on the Piper. The two planes hurtled down the wet runway and threw themselves into the teeth of the storm.

The flight to Rochester was bumpy but without incident. After our visit to a nuclear power plant, we were back at the Rochester airport a few hours later. By now it was dark, and the hail had turned to snow that was blown almost horizontally by winds of over thirty miles per hour, with frequent strong gusts. Our flight plan was to fly east over Syracuse and then to turn southeast toward Hartford, Connecticut, our destination. Our plane had a transponder, allowing air traffic controllers to track us. The controllers' voices came in on a loudspeaker, so all of us could clearly hear them. At our cruising altitude of 6,000 feet, the plane was bobbing around like a cork in the ocean. I had never been tossed around on a plane like that.

The pilot navigated by a map that he was shining his flashlight on and by occasional course corrections from the controllers. "Zero Seven November, you are drifting toward the lake again. Please correct to a heading of ..." From time to time, the pilot shone his flashlight on the edge of the wing, just inches from the cockpit window. That was as far as he could see with snow blowing right at us. Then we heard the pilot send a message to air traffic control that startled the AEC man and me. "This is Zero Seven November. I am getting some icing on my wings. Would you advise an approach to Syracuse?"

"Negative, Zero Seven November. Syracuse is closed. Zero visibility. Surface winds gusting up to eighty miles per hour. Please continue on your present course."

The Austrian seemed to have fallen asleep, either from stress or from advanced age. He was bouncing around in his seat with his eyes closed. In the back, however, we were wide awake, believing that the odds on us crashing or not were now about fifty-fifty. To relieve the tension, we started telling each other airplane crash jokes. James knew one, and I knew two. To our astonishment, we were actually laughing at them, though the pilot kept quiet. We made slow progress because of the strong headwinds, prolonging our mental ordeal. Finally, when we reached the Connecticut border, the temperature rose a couple of degrees, which kept the icing from progressing further.

At last, the flaps came out. A few minutes later, our tires hit the concrete of the runway. We felt like we had just won the lottery and complimented the pilot on his skill and poise. It was a flight that probably never should have taken place. But nuclear power plants are worth millions of dollars. Later, the Swedes won the contract after all and Westinghouse lost out.

I have told the story of this flight in some detail, because it illustrates the essential difference in work environment between the translator and the interpreter. Later in my interpreting career, I experienced a few flights even more harrowing and dangerous than this one, observing drug dealers at the Mexican border and observing military maneuvers. But those dangers pale in comparison to interpreting in wars and uprisings. Even though the number of interpreters on the battlefield is usually insufficient, a considerable number get killed or wounded. When the American media announce their death, they are frequently called "translators," which they are not. Even highly educated journalists and TV anchors make this mistake frequently.

BECOMING A LEGAL EXPERT AND THOROUGHLY ENJOYING IT

During my studies at Mainz University, I had taken some basic courses in law and international law. I had no interest in a career in this field, but knew so little about law and legal terminology that I felt I needed to fill this gap in my general knowledge. A further consideration was that there are many work opportunities for interpreters and translators in the legal field.

In the traveling university of escort interpreting, I had many opportunities to expand that basic knowledge. In 1968 and in 1972, I had the privilege of traveling the United States with two outstanding legal experts, Dr. Hans Klecatsky of Austria and Dr. Diether Posser of Germany. Klecatsky was minister of justice in the Austrian federal government, Posser in the largest German state, North Rhine Westphalia. Both were delightful traveling companions.

In Washington, Dr. Klecatsky met with Associate Supreme Court Justice Potter Stewart and Myrl Alexander, the director of the Bureau of Prisons. We also had a meeting with Attorney General Ramsey Clark and the president of the American Bar Association. Then we flew to Phoenix, rented a car, and drove to Flagstaff, Arizona. It was late April 1968 and the weather was pleasant. The justice minister was handsome, trim, and athletic at age forty-eight, an avid hiker in the Austrian Alps, where he had helped to establish a national park. He had a sunny disposition, was a connoisseur of good wines, and enjoyed playing an occasional practical joke on me.

In Flagstaff, we met with Judge Laurence Wren, who had tried and retried the famous Miranda case, from which the Miranda Rule was born, making law enforcement officers read a person his rights when arresting him. Judge Wren cut our evening meeting short at one point, explaining that he had to get up at five in the morning to go hunting mountain lions.

The next day, we had an appointment with the justice of the peace. After we entered his office, he turned the Open sign on his door to Closed and offered us seats. Klecatsky queried him on the duties of his office in German while I interpreted. The minister had heard from me that there were many Indian reservations nearby and wanted to know if the justice treated Indians differently from other defendants or plaintiffs. The Indians are much easier to deal with, we were told.

He gave an example. A young Navajo man had come off the reservation and had too much to drink at a Flagstaff bar. Roaming the street near the bar at night with two other inebriated Navajos, he had supposedly thrown a stone through somebody's window and smashed a television set. The owner of the TV and the three Navajos had to appear before him. The Indian witnesses refused to answer questions about the incident, as they would not testify against a fellow tribe member outside the reservation. The justice then made the suspect stand in front of him, looked him straight in the eyes, and asked, "White Feather, upon your honor as a Navajo, did you throw that stone through the window?"

"Yes I did," came the quick answer.

"You see," the justice said to us, "White Feather would have been considered a coward if he had lied in front of two other members of the tribe in order to avoid punishment. If you know the Indian customs, they will give you less trouble in court than other people."

We also visited the sheriff of Coconino County, Cecil Richardson. Dr. Klecatsky was impressed with his small but well-equipped crime lab used not only to solve crimes but also to identify skeletons of lost tourists recovered from remote reaches of the Grand Canyon.

The canyon was next on our Arizona itinerary. We spent two days exploring it on foot and by rental car. Although twelve years younger, I had trouble keeping pace with my traveling companion, whose energy seemed to double when out in nature.

May 1, celebrated as Labor Day in Europe, is Law Day USA here. We were in Los Angeles, where Dr. Klecatsky had received an invitation from a German-language radio station to speak to its listeners in the States, Mexico, and South America. A makeshift studio was set up in our hotel. Although I was not needed for a broadcast in German, the minister insisted that I sit next to him. After speaking on the importance of the rule of law and other related matters, he told the audience what he was doing in the United States and thanked our government for the invitation and for having provided him with an interpreter, who "is also a legal expert. Mr. Obst will now speak to you on the occasion of Law Day USA." He shoved the microphone in front of me, looking up at the ceiling with a mischievous smile. He had successfully played another practical joke on me in the middle of a live program, which had five minutes to go.

After assuring the listeners that I was not really a legal expert, I thanked the minister for accepting our invitation to visit the United States. Then I filled the remaining time by talking about the great contributions made to Austrian constitutional law by Dr. Klecatsky and by Austrian expatriate Dr. Hans Kelsen, then a professor emeritus at Stanford University. When the program signed off, he said to me, "I know that this is May 1 and not April 1. But I also knew that you would be able to handle it somehow."

By 1968, the hippie movement was in full swing, especially in California. Antiwar protests, drugs, and free love had become part of the American and Canadian youth culture of the day. In San Francisco, we encountered it in many places. After a visit to a drug rehabilitation clinic in Haight-Ashbury, we were taking a stroll in Golden Gate Park when we came upon a dozen or so young women, wearing nothing from the waist up, with flowers in their hair, dancing to the strains of a flute and a guitar.

That evening, I was showing Chinatown to the Austrian visitor. After walking around for more than an hour, he suggested we have a glass of wine somewhere. From a previous visit, I knew a little bar called Riksha, where a pianist played music and sang for the guests. What I did not know until that evening was that topless waitresses were very common in California that year. We got a nice table. Our waitress was a beautiful young woman, with lustrous black hair and radiant brown eyes. She told the minister, who had asked her whether she was from California, that she was a full-blooded Sioux Indian and had only recently come to San Francisco. But she already knew her way around California wines and suggested a Cabernet Sauvignon that found the minister's full approval. With no more interpreting to do for the day, I had a glass and a half, leaned back, and enjoyed the songs of the pianist. For the moment, escort interpreting did not look like such a daunting task.

However, interpreting became much more difficult a couple of days later during discussions with leading faculty members at Harvard and Tufts universities in Massachusetts. The subjects were the role of law in economic development and problems of constitutional law. What had been phrased by the attorney general and by Associate Justice Potter Stewart in clear and straightforward legal English, now came at me with many strange twists and turns of academic parlance. Occasionally, I just could not understand the point being made and had to ask a follow-up question to untangle the web that I could not penetrate. I was glad when we got out of there for a visit with the mayor of Boston.

The justice minister was the only independent member of Bruno Kreisky's Socialist party cabinet. His personal philosophy, however, was conservative. In Arizona, he had regretted that Senator Barry Goldwater, who had run against Lyndon Johnson and lost in the 1964 presidential election, was out of town. He would have loved to meet him.

At the end of the trip, we were visiting New York City. I read in the *New York Times* that Goldwater was in town as a plaintiff in federal court against the publisher Ralph Ginzburg, whom he had accused of libel.

I took Dr. Klecatsky to the court to sit in on the trial. When the judge called a recess, it so happened that Goldwater came walking down the aisle near our seats. I quickly got up and asked him if he would like to meet the minister of justice of Austria. The senator, for whom I had once interpreted in Washington, readily agreed. The two had a brief conversation in which Klecatsky told Goldwater that he had always admired him. To the Austrian, this brief encounter was one of the highlights of his study tour, which came to an end in New York; from there, he flew back to Vienna.

WATERGATE AND THE WAR OF NORTHERN AGRESSION

I had first met Diether Posser a year before his arrival in August of 1972 as a grantee of the International Visitor Program. In fact, our first encounter led to the second. Before the 1980s, staff interpreters at Language Services in Washington had few opportunities to work in simultaneous interpretation, but when we were called to do so it often was important and sensitive work. To keep us from getting rusty, the State Department permitted us to moonlight occasionally at private conferences, provided we did so over weekends or when using a couple of days of our annual leave.

The Christian Conference on Arms Control and Disarmament, a private international organization, held a meeting in the United States over the three-day Labor Day weekend in September of 1971. I received an offer to interpret from English into German. Though we had interpreting booths and good equipment, the venue was anything but ideal. The conference took place at a seminary in Massachusetts that had no air-conditioning. The weather was very hot and humid. Inside the closed booths, the mid-day temperature was in the upper nineties. Two women interpreters were working in their underwear, with bath towels from the hotel draped loosely over their bodies to ensure propriety and absorb the perspiration.

Dr. Posser was one of a number of delegates from different countries who spoke no English. He had to depend on listening to my and my booth-mate's translation. He came to our booth as the conference was winding down and complimented me on my interpretation. This led to a brief conversation later in the day in which he told me a few things about himself. He was a cabinet member in the largest German state, with a population of more than 16 million, but had never been to our country before. He also told me that his former law partner and fellow politician, Gustav Heinemann, had been treated rudely during his only visit to the United States during the McCarthy era, when Socialists were often equated with Communists. Nobody would see him in Washington except Lyndon Johnson, at the time a senator from Texas, who always had a warm spot for Germans in his heart.

The Christian Democratic Union (CDU) was the dominant political party under Konrad Adenauer, Germany's first postwar chancellor. Most of its members were Catholics, though most Germans then were (and still are) Protestants. Heinemann and Posser founded a Protestant-oriented Christian political party, called *Gesamtdeutsche Volkspartei,* as a counterweight to the CDU. Their party later was absorbed into the Social Democratic party (SPD), out of which Willy Brandt, Helmut Schmidt, and Gerhard Schröder emerged as chancellors, and Gustav Heinemann and Johannes Rau, another close friend of Diether Posser, became presidents of Germany.

It appeared obvious that Posser was an ideal candidate for the International Visitor Program. After he had returned from the conference to Germany, I contacted our ambassador in Bonn, Martin Hillenbrand, and suggested that the embassy might want to invite him. This was done. Posser gladly accepted and requested me as his interpreter.

As there were many parallels between Klecatsky and Posser, there were also many differences. Both were strongly interested in the legal foundations of the political systems of their countries and how they compared to other countries. Both had brilliant minds and the courage to take action and become involved. At the time I traveled with them, Klecatsky was quick, nimble, and lively, and had the build of a professional tennis player. Posser had the physique of a football lineman and was cautious and circumspect, an uncommonly keen observer who took his good time before rendering judgment on anything. He also was a religious, self-effacing, and generous man.

Posser successively held three different cabinet posts in North Rhine Westphalia: minister for federal affairs, minister of finance, and minister of justice. When he arrived in Washington in 1972, he was in charge of finance. However, he was more interested in the American political system, social issues, and our system of justice. Like Heinemann, he hailed from Essen, once a polluted town of Krupp steel factories and coal mines, today a clean metropolis, a cultural center, and a mecca for shoppers with its many well-stocked and reasonably priced stores. Essen immediately built a bridge between the two of us. I had worked there as a coal miner after escaping from East Germany, had completed my high school studies in the town, and had brought my mother and sister there after their own later escape from communism.

Traveling with Posser was a pleasure. He was courteous, never made unreasonable demands, treated me like an equal, and was insatiably curious. No other visitor asked me as many questions about the United States. And once I had given an answer, he would never forget it, including facts, dates, and names. He seemed to have the memory of two elephants. When I expressed an opinion on anything, he would absorb it with several grains of salt and wait for developments or other voices to confirm it. He quickly realized that I grasped certain things intuitively rather than from careful and prolonged observation and would often render judgment based on that intuition and former experiences. He did not much care for this method of forming opinions.

When I took him sightseeing in Washington, we drove by the Watergate residential and office complex on Virginia Avenue. I told him about the break-in at McGovern's presidential campaign headquarters on June 17, less than two months earlier. None of the revelations by Woodward and Bernstein had appeared as yet. It was still a mystery.

"Dr. Posser, this will become one of the biggest scandals in the history of the United States," I said to him.

"How can you make such an assumption?" he retorted indignantly.

"From what I know about Washington," I replied, "no one could have had a motive for breaking into that office other than the people around President Nixon. The trail will lead to the White House sooner or later, and then all hell will break loose."

He just shook his head with an incredulous smile.

Despite our opposite styles, we began to learn a lot from each other. I learned about judicial systems, German politics, and the details of events in history. Like Helmut Kohl, with whom I often worked, Posser knew his history. He also was a generalist par excellence. There was virtually nothing that did not interest him, that he had not explored or read about at one time or another. He, in turn, learned from me about the nature, structure, and cultural peculiarities of the United States, particularly what was different from Europe, because as an immigrant from Europe, I had a good basis of comparison. We were both students and teachers at the same time.

After a week of appointments in Washington, we set out for Columbia, South Carolina. When we arrived at the Capitol Building for an appointment, Posser, ever the keen observer, noticed, before I did, that the Confederate flag was flying from the top of it. He asked me how that was possible. Was South Carolina not a full-fledged state of the federation? Did it have a special status like Puerto Rico? I responded that, 110 years later, for many people in the South, the Civil War was not completely over, that it still colored their thinking and was a fixture of their homes and surroundings. There also were numerous rebel flags on graves in a nearby cemetery.

Even better proof for my answer came on the next day. We went to Charleston and were taken on a sight-seeing tour by a local volunteer for the International Visitor Program, Mrs. Quattlebaum. She was white-haired, probably in her eighties, and of patrician appearance and dress. The lady showed us a number of mansions. She would say, "This mansion was built twenty years after the War of Northern Aggression." Whenever she referred to the Civil War, and that was often, it was the War of Northern Aggression. A few days later, in Atlanta, we had a few similar experiences. Feelings of pride in the Southern cause and bitterness about losing the war to the North had been passed on from generation to generation and were only declining at a slow pace.

HOW MANY TRIPS DOES IT TAKE TO GET TO KNOW THE UNITED STATES?

From Atlanta, we took a quantum leap to the West to Las Vegas, the Grand Canyon, Carmel, and San Francisco. I had told Posser earlier that I never took an umbrella with me to Las Vegas, because I had never encountered a day of rain there. Famous last words! When we got off the airplane, it was pouring cats and dogs. Some streets were flooded and closed to traffic. It took twice as long as usual to get to our hotel.

The next day, though, when we took Scenic Airlines to the Grand Canyon, the sun was back out. It is interesting to note that virtually all visitors from Germany, when asked at the beginning of their trip by the program planner where they would like to go, named the Grand Canyon, Niagara Falls, New Orleans, and San Francisco, or at least two of the four. Hardly anybody ever asked for Yosemite, Yellowstone, or Chicago. These places, in addition to New York City, seemed linked in the German mind to our country. The trip planners, who only had a limited number of days available to cover each visitor's professional and substantive study agenda, usually tried to keep those requests to a minimum. Once some visitors sensed the reluctance to accommodate such requests, they would press harder to get some of those places on their itinerary. This sometimes led to a hilarious linguistic misunderstanding. Most visitors, although needing an interpreter, had acquired a limited amount of English in their high school classes. It so happens that the German adverb *eventuell* means "maybe" in English. When the trip planner would say, "We will go to New York, Boston, Chicago, and eventually to San Francisco," the visitor would excitedly interrupt and insist that he *must* go to San Francisco, not "eventually."

Another German/English linguistic misunderstanding sometimes happened when in a high-rise building with a sizeable group of visitors. If you were on the seventeenth floor of a sixty-story building and finished your appointment, you would need to get the group back down to the lobby. If an upward-bound elevator stopped on your floor, the door would open and the operator would say, "Up!" A number of the visitors might pile into the cab and ignore the interpreter's pleading to come back out. Off they'd go, toward the sixtieth floor. The reason is that the operators in Germany shout, "*Ab!*" for "Down," and it is pronounced exactly like "up."

As Klecatsky had done, Posser also visited a drug rehabilitation clinic in Haight-Ashbury when we were in San Francisco. How to fight the problem of drug addiction had occupied his mind for a long time. We met some heroin addicts who were now on methadone, with limited success. A young woman in her twenties, who had abused heroin since she was thirteen, looked about fifty years older, just skin and bones and wrinkles all over.

We had a long discussion afterwards. Posser told me that heroin was actually named for the heroes of war and had been marketed by Bayer to combat morphine addiction in soldiers. However, it was discovered later that the liver just converted this synthetic opiate back into a form of morphine. Heroin became useless for its intended purpose. Both of us were in agreement that hunting down and imprisoning drug dealers was counterproductive. They can earn such huge amounts of money that any dealer, taken out of circulation, will immediately be replaced by someone else, thus the trade continues unabated. At the clinic, we had just been told what we had heard and read before: that rehabilitation works only for a few. Most addicts will stay addicted, even if switched to a different narcotic. Diether came to the conclusion that government money to fight drug addiction would be most effectively spent on prevention. If young people could be graphically shown the ravages their bodies would suffer from taking hard drugs, many might be persuaded not to get into this habit, despite peer pressure.

Posser had wished to visit a ranch. From Denver, we took a small two-engine propeller plane to Steamboat Springs, Colorado. From my seat, I could see directly through the open cockpit door and watch the pilots. When we were over Boulder, I noticed an orange sign flashing in the cockpit. I looked at it through the telescopic lens of my camera. The sign read "ENGINE ON FIRE." The copilot pulled out a hose and started to blow into it. I thought he might be blowing a fire retardant into the engine. Getting concerned, I alerted Posser to the problem and told him to be prepared for a possible rapid descent into Boulder. Posser sniffed the cabin like a rabbit. "I can smell neither smoke nor fire. Don't worry." He was right. The incident blew over, and we landed safely at Steamboat Springs.

From there, we drove to the picturesque Fetcher Ranch on the Elk River, where we were invited to stay at the ranch house with the family. The conversation around the dinner table revolved around Germany and the excitement that the 1976 Winter Olympics had been awarded to Denver, with nearby Steamboat Springs to build sites for some of the events. Fetcher was on the committee preparing the sites and gave each of us a pin with the emblem of the Denver Olympics, which were never to take place. Shortly after our visit, the people of Colorado voted against funding the games for ecological reasons. Innsbruck, Austria, the city where Peggy Fleming, whom I had escorted to a White House dinner in 1965, had won the gold medal for figure skating in 1964, then volunteered to take the games again.

The Fetcher family, in contrast to most Americans living in the middle of the country, was interested in foreign countries and frequently invited guests from around the globe. They were courteous and lively hosts whose company we enjoyed as much as the mountains, the animals, and the Elk River Valley.

From the Fetcher Ranch we went to Pittsburgh, a city whose past economy had much in common with Posser's hometown of Essen: coal and steel. There I received an order from the State Department to go to Baton Rouge, Louisiana, to interpret at a conference. Another interpreter was sent to take Posser to New York, and we had to part company.

Posser knew that, at that time, I had lived in the United States for nine years. As I was saying good-bye to him, he asked me one more question: "How many thirty-day trips does it take to get a firm grip on what the United States is like?"

I paused a minute to think this over and replied, "For a keen observer like you, it would probably take five such trips."

This answer was totally unscientific. Once again, it was pulled from my intuition and based on my previous experiences. Little did I know that Posser would accept this as a credible baseline.

In the next twenty years, Posser would make ten private trips to the United States, some coast-to-coast roundtrips with itineraries incorporating my suggestions. Once his English had improved and he felt more comfortable, he would bring his wife and other relatives along, becoming a guide to America himself. Few Germans ever got to know the United States as well as Diether Posser. We became friends and frequently visited each other on both sides of the Atlantic. I took him to see friends of mine. He introduced me to two of his best friends, Gustav Heinemann and Johannes Rau. I visited both of them in Berlin when they were president of Germany. Heinemann quizzed me on the United States for almost three hours. What puzzled him the most was that some American judges are elected by the voters, in Texas, for instance. A lawyer and judicial expert himself, he did not believe that such judges could be as impartial as they should be.

The invitation to Diether Posser to come and visit the United States turned out to have a considerable multiplier effect. Foreigners invited under the International Visitor Program do not just learn about the country, its culture, and its people. They make friends here. They establish professional contacts that last. Some come back to visit again. They talk to many of their own countrymen about their experiences. Some, like Posser, write about it in their local newspapers. The program builds many bridges of mutual understanding and removes wrong notions that can lead to conflicts between countries.

Nobody knows that better than the escort interpreters, who also make some friends for life from among the visitors. During my thirty-two years with the Department of State, funding for the program occasionally experienced deep cuts, usually under Republican administrations. The argument was frequently floated that it is stupid to finance trips for foreigners when they do not reciprocate by inviting Americans to tour their countries for free. What the proponents of this notion overlook, among many other American benefits of the program, is that Americans, too, learn a lot from the foreigners who visit here. Americans in many regions have precious little knowledge about what goes on in other parts of the world. Even the names and locations of many nations are not familiar to them. In the middle of the cold war, visitors I escorted into Louisiana, Texas, and New Mexico, to name but three states, encountered Americans who were astonished to hear that Germany was divided into two entirely different parts and that there was such a thing as the Berlin Wall. They had never heard of it. It took them a while to understand that the Austrian visitors were not from Australia. The teaching function of the small traveling university of escorting foreigners reaches beyond the visitors and their interpreters. It benefits many others.

PRESIDENTIAL VIGNETTES

RONALD W. REAGAN

1981–1989

COMMUNICATING THE GREAT COMMUNICATOR

In the fall of 1980, many Washington pundits were predicting that Carter would win a narrow reelection victory, despite rampant inflation in the wake of a gigantic spike in oil prices and several foreign-policy setbacks. I held the same opinion until I spent several days west of the Mississippi River, as interpreter for Dr. Juergen Starnick, president of the Technical University of Berlin. The subject of the elections came up in almost every business meeting and encounter we had with American experts and private citizens. Out West, even in California, I could scarcely find anybody willing to vote for Carter. He was incredibly unpopular and Reagan's stock was riding high, especially in Texas and California, two economic and political powerhouses with many electoral votes.

A few weeks after my return, I found myself in the backseat of a limousine on the way to Capitol Hill, seated next to Klaus Bölling. He was then the spokesman of the German government under Chancellor Schmidt, whom I had often interpreted for since the late sixties, when he was a German member of parliament. I told Bölling about my experience out West. "Ronald Reagan will win easily," I said to him. "Maybe you should tell the chancellor to get ready for a change in Washington."

Bölling gave me an amused glance. He knew that he was talking to an American interpreter, not to anyone of importance in Washington. "I will do no such thing," he replied. "We are preparing for a second Carter administration."

The morning of November 4, 1980, I went to my polling place to vote for Jimmy Carter anyhow, even though I was dead sure that he would lose. I took a very dim view of Reagan's economic philosophy. If I had learned anything in the many years I had been in Washington, from the many meetings with top economic experts at which I had interpreted, from the G7 economic summits I had attended, it was what works well for the U.S. economy and what does not.

The Laffer curve, supply-side economics, tax cuts for the wealthy to produce a "trickle down effect," in my opinion, would not propel the economy forward. Building and maintaining economic infrastructure, maintaining a well-off middle class to stimulate consumption, supporting the small and medium-sized businesses that create millions of new jobs (while the big corporations dismiss tens of thousands at the drop of a hat to better balance the quarterly financial reports), those initiatives I had learned by now provide positive stimuli in a free-market economy. Two economic experts who had strengthened my convictions in this regard had been two German chancellors: Ludwig Erhard and Helmut Schmidt.

None of those elements were in Reagan's plan. Even the fellow Republican who was to become his vice president, George Bush, had called this approach "voodoo economics." I wholeheartedly shared that view.

Later that evening, I was on an airplane in a right window seat, looking down on the lights of Chattanooga, Tennessee. I was on my way to Huntsville, Alabama, to interpret at a military meeting on a missile system we were building jointly with the French, the Germans, and the British. The polls on the West Coast were still open when, at 8:27 pm EST, the pilot came on the loudspeaker and told us that two of the major television networks had just declared Reagan the winner of the election. That clearly indicated that it had to be a landslide, and it was. Reagan won forty-four states, Carter only six, plus the District of Columbia.

For the rest of the plane ride, I was wondering what working for my fifth president would be like. I had interpreted for him as governor of California two or three times. He had been very courteous and friendly toward me. Certainly he would not be another Nixon, who had also been a Republican from California. In Sacramento, he had been easy to understand by word and body language, something interpreters welcome, as it makes their job much easier. The press label "the Great Communicator" fit him well. A fervent anticommunist myself, I liked his hard line vis-à-vis the Soviet Union and his determination not to let them overtake us militarily. But the world at large and the United States in particular were in a precarious position in 1980. Could a former movie actor and sports announcer safely steer our ship through those turbulent waters? I had a few doubts.

GETTING APPLAUSE TWICE

Under Nixon, interpreters often had been distrusted and occasionally even mistreated. Under Carter, in reaction to the president's overblown interpreting mishap during his arrival in Warsaw in December 1977, we State Department interpreters had been given access to the White House speechwriters for the first time and were occasionally asked advice by the president or his assistants. When I arrived at the White House for my first mission with Ronald Reagan, I was taken aside by an aide and admonished never to speak to the president privately, only to answer questions that he might ask.

Presidents and interpreters often have to work as a team, especially on the public stage, in an exercise that seasoned interpreters know a great deal more about than new occupants of the White House. Discussing certain logistics with the president ahead of time, when the interpreter, from professional experience, anticipates a problem, is of benefit to all parties concerned, especially the president. I quietly resolved not to pay any attention to this admonition unless it were to be given directly to me by a principal assistant, like Jim Baker, Ed Meese, or Mike Deaver, and they never did.

Anytime an interpreter can give some helpful advice to a president, he should do it, just as his press secretary or chief of protocol would. Low-level aides often do not understand the intricacies of efficient interpreting and frequently prevent the smooth functioning of the process in their myopic, though well-meaning, zeal. They usually do not know that professional interpreters are just as well educated as they are.

Chancellor Helmut Kohl welcomes President Reagan before a meeting in Bonn. *Photo courtesy of German Foreign Office*

On my first trip to Europe with President Reagan, he was to give a major speech to 25,000 Berliners assembled on the lawn behind Charlottenburg Castle on June 11, 1982. President Karl Carstens and Chancellor Schmidt had gone with us from Bonn, then the capital of the Federal Republic of Germany, and were to speak ahead of Reagan, as was the governing mayor of Berlin. The plan was for me to whisper a simultaneous translation of their remarks into the president's left ear, as he was somewhat hard of hearing in his right ear. Then he and I would proceed to separate sets of microphones on the elevated podium, facing the crowd and television cameras from several countries. I would do a consecutive translation of his keynote speech into German.

Ten minutes before the event, I was chatting with Germany's chief interpreter, Heinz Weber, by then an old friend, and with Hans-Jürgen Wischnewski, a German cabinet member from East Prussia, where I, too, was born. He was also known by the nickname "Ben Wisch," because he was an expert on and frequent government contact with the Arab world.

Suddenly, two Secret Service agents marched up to our group, while Wischnewski was talking to us. The younger agent pointed a finger at me and rudely barked, "You, come with me!" The Germans were startled by such impolite behavior, and I was angry to be summoned like a criminal about to be arrested. "The hell I will," I retorted, equally curtly. Before I could say much more, the older agent pushed his younger colleague aside and said, "Gentlemen, excuse us for interrupting your conversation. Mr. Obst, the president would like to have a word with you. Please follow me."

We went down a corridor in the castle and the agent opened a door, motioned me inside, and closed it behind me. Nancy Reagan was sitting in front of a mirror in a pretty white dress, adjusting her hair, and the president was pacing up and down nervously, staring at four-by-six speech cards. The scene was like a dressing room for two movie actors, five minutes before stepping onto the set. I went up to Reagan and said, "Mr. President, you sent for me?"

"Yes, this speech that we have to do together. I have been thinking about it. I will give you a sentence or half a sentence at a time and then give you a chance to interpret."

"With all due respect, Mr. President, I do not think that is a good idea."

The First Lady spun around in her chair and stared at me disapprovingly. Maybe it startled her that such a low-ranking person would dare to disagree with the president. I had heard that she was very protective of her husband.

President Reagan and Harry Obst discuss interpreting strategy before a joint appearance in Berlin (June 11, 1982). *White House photo*

Reagan also looked surprised, took a step back, and said, "Well, what do you mean?"

"Mr. President, you are an excellent speaker and this speech will be carried all over on television. If you stop every sentence or half-sentence, it will chop up your delivery and you will not sound good. I would suggest that you do two or three sentences at a time before stopping for interpretation."

"You mean three or four cards?"

"Yes sir, if that makes about three sentences. But, as you well know, for every rule there is an exception."

"Well, what would that be?"

"Please give me two or three sentences unless you get interrupted by applause. Stop in the middle of a sentence if the crowd applauds and let me interpret right away."

"Well, why should I do that?"

"Mr. President, half of the crowd understands the English and the other half does not. If I can interpret right away, you will then get applause again from the other half of the crowd."

Reagan cracked a little smile and said, "Okay. Let's do it that way."

We did, and it worked just as predicted. So what is wrong with giving a president a little advice?

DARK CLOUD IN THE JUNE SKY

During Reagan's very successful visit to Europe, of which Germany was the last stop, we also had a last meeting with Chancellor Helmut Schmidt in his office. Nobody knew that his administration would not last another three months, but everybody knew that it was in trouble, especially the chancellor himself. Under the chairmanship of former chancellor Willy Brandt, the Social Democratic party had veered too far to the left, losing the confidence not only of many German voters, but even more so of the Free Democrats, who were governing in coalition with the SPD. This was the party of his highly skilled foreign minister, Hans-Dietrich Genscher, who also held the office of vice chancellor.

I had known Schmidt since the late sixties and often admired his vigor, action-oriented optimism, and razor-sharp mind when it came to analyzing problems. Nothing seemed to escape his attention, but he could also be laid back and charming, as he was during the Puerto Rico Economic Summit.

Like Willy Brandt, Schmidt had a good command of English. Strangely enough, the quality of his English seemed to be a function of his physical condition. When he was rested and feeling well, his English was fine. When he was tired or ailing, his English faltered immediately. Knowing this, he always liked to have an interpreter around.

One day, Schmidt was in Washington and had a meeting scheduled with President Carter and National Security Adviser Zbigniew Brzezinski. I was told the day before that no interpreting was needed for that meeting. From previous experience, I knew that things can change, so I put on a dark suit and tie in the morning, just in case. When I was having lunch in the huge State Department cafeteria, I heard my name called out. It was Susan Klingaman, then the German desk officer at State, walking around the cafeteria, calling out my name in all directions. When she found me, she said the White House had just called her. Schmidt wanted me to be in the meeting. It would start in about twenty minutes. I left my lunch and barely got to the Oval Office in time.

The meeting proceeded in English for twenty minutes or so. Never needed, I was half asleep when Schmidt suddenly turned to me and wanted the translation of a German word. The word was unexpected, and in my stupor I could not understand it. I asked the chancellor to repeat it. He bellowed out loud, "*Hühnchenfutter.*" This time I understood and replied, "chicken feed." Brzezinski pointed a finger at me and said, "Not with this president, Mr. Obst. The correct term is 'peanuts.'" Everybody had a good laugh, because we all knew that Carter had been a peanut farmer in his past.

Meeting with Schmidt had always been interesting and invigorating. But when I entered his office that June with President Reagan, Ed Meese, and George Shultz, I was in shock.

There were no photos or paintings on the walls, with one exception. Behind his desk hung a painting showing an ominous dark storm over a violently churning sea. It was almost frightening to look at. And Schmidt was almost frightening to listen to. He dwelt on the world's biggest problems: Russian missiles, poverty and disease in Africa and elsewhere, growing economic disparities between nations, and so on. It was a depressing panoply of doom and gloom, without his usual pointing to possible solutions. This was no longer the Helmut Schmidt I had known before. Maybe he had sunk into deep depression. I do not know how the other Americans felt about this meeting. I never heard them comment on it. But I left sad, like someone who had just attended a funeral.

BITBURG AND HAMBACH CASTLE

Three years later, in May 1985, President Reagan was in Germany again, now ruled by the Christian Democrat Helmut Kohl, also in coalition with the Free Democrats. Hans-Dietrich Genscher was still the foreign minister. He held this post continuously for eighteen years. Only one other foreign minister ever served longer in world history: Andrei Gromyko of the Soviet Union, who holds the record at twenty-eight years.

By now, I was the director of the Office of Language Services and was only interpreting occasionally. My talented staff colleague Gisela Marcuse had taken over the bulk of high-level German interpreting. On this trip, there was too much interpreting for one person, so we split the duties. Gisela went to Bonn and to Bergen-Belsen to cover Reagan's visit to the former concentration camp, while I went ahead to Bitburg Airbase, where Reagan and Kohl were to make solemn remarks after Bergen-Belsen, and the subsequent controversial visit to Bitburg Cemetery, where Nazi followers lie buried next to American and Allied soldiers who fell in World War II. The day was supposed to be a remembrance of the horrors under Hitler as well as a day of reconciliation as part of the fortieth anniversary commemoration of the end of the war.

When I arrived at the airbase, I got a quick lesson that diplomatic activities should not be left to the military. Inspecting the platform in front of a hangar where the speeches were to be given two hours later, I found some young lieutenants, just out of the Air Force Academy, making the protocol arrangements. They had arrayed two groups of folding chairs in four rows, one for the American party, one for the Germans. Except for Reagan and Kohl, they did not know the rank behind peoples' names. Cabinet members were seated in the back, low-ranking people in the first row. They were very indignant when I moved the seating cards according to proper protocol order.

On the back of the American chairs, there was a pretty silver and black sign, reading "Official Party." On the back of each German chair, there was a similar sign, reading *"Offizielle Amtliche Partei."* Translating this back into English, this means something like "Officially Sanctioned Political Party." The German word *Partei* never carries the second meaning of *delegation*, as the English word does. The German press would have had a field day with those signs.

The lieutenants rebelled when I wanted those signs removed and possibly replaced by "Deutsche Delegation." They pointed out that the translation had been done by the official airbase translator. Therefore, it had to be correct. Here was another sad example of the quality of so many American translators who never had professional training. I had to summon the colonel in charge. After I explained the situation, he ordered the signs removed and thanked me for rearranging the seating.

More embarrassment was ahead. The Air Force had assembled a respectable number of spectators, consisting mostly of military men and their families. They had to be in place two hours before the beginning of the ceremony. To keep them entertained, there was unlimited free beer, hot dogs, and hamburgers. By the time the president and the chancellor arrived for their solemn speeches dealing with concentration camps and war casualties, too much beer had been consumed and part of the crowd had become unruly. It was a county fair atmosphere, unsuitable for the purpose at hand. A somber-looking Reagan was greeted with loud cheers of "Hi, Ronnie!" The German chancellor was almost totally ignored. This event was definitely not a diplomatic success.

The next day found us at Hambach Castle, where things went much better. In May 1832, a number of Germans, many of them young and idealistic, had assembled at this castle at a festival calling for a unified and democratic country. It was the overture presaging the unsuccessful revolution of 1848.

Here, Reagan was scheduled to make a speech to young Germans. He was preceded by Bernhard Vogel, governor of the State of Rhineland-Palatinate, where the castle is located and where Helmut Kohl, also present, once had been governor. The president and I were sitting alone together while Nancy Reagan was seated with Hannelore Kohl, several feet away. He was glancing over his fairly lengthy speech, alluding in part to German historical sites and persons of the nineteenth century, while I was whispering a translation of Vogel's remarks into his ear. As Vogel's speech moved along, mentioning some of the same people and sites, Reagan seemed to get somewhat agitated. Finally, he turned to me and complained, "He is stealing my thunder."

"I would not worry about it," I replied. "The young people probably are not even listening to him. They came here to hear the president of the United States. If the governor is mentioning some of the same historic events, he is only validating what is in your speech."

"Well, I hope you are right," mumbled Reagan.

Minutes later, he mounted the podium and delivered a spirited speech that drew much applause.

JOKES IN PLACE OF PORCELAIN ELEPHANTS

Ronald Reagan loved to tell jokes from his endless repertoire. He was a born entertainer. Jokes are always a problem for interpreters, because the humor can often lose a lot of punch when replicated in another language for people used to a different culture of what is considered funny. Conversely, jokes are easy to remember for interpreters, because they are based on the anticipation of a punch line. Anticipation is one of the techniques used by interpreters to remember better.

When the word got around foreign leaders that the American president was very fond of jokes, they would sometimes bring a good joke as a present to the White House, rather than an elephant or eagle made of wood or china.

One day we had a working lunch at the White House with Chancellor Kohl and Foreign Minister Genscher. The two were seated across from me, as I had pulled up a chair between Reagan and Vice President George Bush. Genscher told the president that he had brought a joke for him that he had recently heard in Budapest. The long joke, which did not lose much in translation, went something like this:

For the first time ever, the Romanian President Ceausescu had to host a meeting of the Warsaw Pact leaders, and he was nervous about it. He called in his chief of protocol and told him that he wanted to host an impressive banquet. Every time he had gone to the Kremlin, Warsaw, or Budapest, the tables had been laid out with exquisite sets of silver.

He told the chief to find the finest set of silverware and report back to him next morning.

The next morning, the chief returned and reported that in the Historical Museum, there was a large chest of genuine gold tableware. Had any of the other leaders ever laid the table out in gold?

"No," replied Ceausescu, and he wrote an order to the museum to release the set. When the leaders sat down for the banquet, they were greatly impressed and complimented the beaming Romanian president on his choice of tableware. Long after the soup, as dessert was being served, Brezhnev was looking down the table to his left and noticed that Prime Minister Gierek, two chairs over, had picked up his golden soup spoon and was stuffing it in his jacket pocket. His first reaction was that as the president of the Warsaw Pact, he should not permit this and should call him on it. But then a little voice in him said that nobody liked the Romanians anyhow. The voice also reminded him that the Brezhnev family never owned even a golden teaspoon.

If Gierek could get away with it, so could he. He waited until nobody was looking, and reached for his soup spoon. Being an older man, his hand was not very dexterous, and he accidentally banged the spoon against his water glass. Everybody fell silent and looked at him, expecting a toast.

Leonid, you must think quickly now, he alerted himself. Then he lifted his spoon up high and said, "Comrades, you probably think that I want to make a speech. But that is not so. Look at this spoon in my hand. It reminds me of a magic trick I used to do in high school. I will put this spoon in my right jacket pocket, and before any of you can count to ten, I will pull it out of Gierek's right jacket pocket."

Reagan and Bush roared with laughter. They would not have gotten half as much pleasure out of a porcelain elephant.

LECTURING ON THE UNITED STATES AND REAGAN IN GERMANY

In September of 1979, the governor of Baden-Württemberg, Lothar Späth, made a whirlwind tour of the United States, accompanied by a group of journalists and the executive secretary of the *Juniorenkreise der Deutschen Wirtschaft*, the German equivalent of our Young Republicans. When the group was discussing American phenomena like labor unions, political parties, taxation by state governments, and primary elections during our air travel between cities, their descriptions were often far off the mark. One job of an escort interpreter is to explain the American scene to foreign visitors. Quite a few times, they asked me for clarification or I simply spoke up and corrected the facts. For instance, they believed that most American workers were unionized, because more than 80 percent of the German workers were at that time. When I told them that about 75 percent of American workers were not in unions, most of them did not believe me.

At that time, I was at the peak of my professional interpreting skills. This sometimes made the group's German interpreter, Gordon Campbell from Stuttgart, feel terribly inferior. Remembering how considerately I had been treated by Heinz Weber early in my career, I virtually never corrected Gordon and treated him as an equal. After the trip, he wrote in a letter to me, "I am sincerely indebted to you, not least for the generosity and courtesy with which you handled me—a mere cub in this field."

When later checking by the group confirmed that I had my facts straight and that their knowledge of the United States had many significant gaps, it led to an invitation by the *Juniorenkreise* to come to Germany sometime and lecture on the United States, especially on the political and economic scene. My first tour of about five lectures each trip was to Baden-Württemberg, where I spoke in Singen, near Lake Constance, on a rain-soaked evening in November of 1981.

Much to my surprise, the lecture hall, despite the terrible weather, was so crowded that a side room had to be opened to accommodate everybody. This buoyed my spirits, and the presentation went well. During the discussion that followed, it turned out that the local Communists had smuggled in two provocateurs who kept denigrating everything American and praising the Soviet Union where, according to them, people lived happily without crime, exploitation, and unemployment. From watching skilled politicians like Hubert Humphrey, I had learned how to neutralize such troublemakers with smiles, wit, and humor, rather than meeting their arguments with confrontational counter-fire.

The audience warmed to that approach, rewarding me with so much laughter and applause that the provocateurs quickly fell silent.

By accident, a journalist from the *Frankfurter Allgemeine*, a leading national newspaper, was at the lecture. He asked whether I had a biographical sketch and a photo in my briefcase, and I did. He wrote me up for their bio page with the headline "*Die Stimme Amerikas*," "The Voice of America." This article and the success of the first series led to several other invitations to lecture in Germany. In the following years, I would take a week of annual leave every year or two and speak in different parts of Germany.

I never speak without allowing at least fifteen to twenty minutes for questions. It is a good way of finding out whether you have reached the audience or not. In the early eighties, the subject of Ronald Reagan came up repeatedly. His immense popularity in the States was rarely matched in Europe.

Speaking always as a private citizen, of course, invited by private German associations, I found myself in the curious position to be criticizing or praising the president I was still working for—a delicate task. I criticized the enormous expansion of the federal debt, the lack of oversight over banks and savings institutions, the impoverishment of the middle class, and the coddling of the wealthy and the big corporations. I bemoaned the lack of building economic infrastructure, apart from defense establishments, and some other policies.

But I was also a determined defender of the president, especially in the area of foreign policy. One city where I had agreed to speak in early November of 1983 was Recklinghausen in Germany's most populous state of North Rhine-Westphalia, a stronghold of the Social Democratic party. It was supposed to be a presentation on the political and economic scene in the United States. But when I got off the train to take a taxi to the lecture hall, there were several yellow posters announcing that I would hold a debate with the political editor of the *Westfälische Rundschau* that evening. That newspaper was sort of the national house organ of the Social Democratic party, at that time in opposition to Chancellor Kohl. Nobody had informed me of that, and I sensed that a trap had been set for me to catch me unprepared.

My first reaction was that I should not walk into that trap and cancel out. I had never done a public political debate beyond answering questions after my presentations. But by the time I reached the lecture hall, the unexpected challenge and my curiosity about whether I could adequately handle it or not got the better of me. However, once on the podium, I told the moderator of the debate, who was sitting between me and the editor, that this was not what I had agreed on and what I had prepared for. I was only going along with it because the hall was full and I did not want to disappoint the audience. This was a defensive move and amounted to an advance apology to the audience, in case I did not do well. Sure enough, the topics were introduced in a manner that did not throw a good light on the United States and on Reagan, the moderator displayed his own bias, and the editor had carefully crafted a good deal of criticism of Reagan's foreign policy.

President Mikhail Gorbachev signs President Reagan's guestbook in December 1987, as the two principal interpreters Pavel Palazchenko (in front of clock) and Dimitri Zarechnak (U.S. Department of State) are watching. *White House photo*

The most heated topic of the evening was our invasion of Grenada, which had just happened after I left Washington. What I knew about it was from reading the *Neue Zürcher Zeitung*, a Swiss newspaper that, when it comes to the accuracy of facts, is one of the best in the world. The German editor's version was very much at variance with those facts. He never mentioned that the Cubans were building a large military airfield there, nor how brutally Prime Minister Maurice Bishop, members of his government, and members of their families had been murdered in the Communist coup. Nor did he mention that the chairwoman of the Organization of Eastern Caribbean States, Prime Minister Eugenia Charles, had called Reagan and asked the United States for help. Reagan had another motive to intervene: hundreds of American medical students were on the island and needed to be evacuated.

The Swiss paper had provided me with some other interesting facts, for instance, that the new Soviet ambassador to Grenada was a four-star general. I asked the audience if they believed that a great military power like the Soviet Union would send one of their best generals to a small speck of a Caribbean island unless some significant military project was underfoot there. I contradicted the editor's assertion that a U.S.-dominated government would be installed by the United States, making Grenada another "American banana republic." I predicted that our troops would be out in a few months and that a local democratic government would quickly be in place. I was sure that Reagan would have no interest in an American Grenada, once the Cubans had been ousted. Grenada did not interest him; stopping the export of Castro's revolution did.

Surprisingly, the very liberal audience responded to my arguments. My responses to the questions got more applause than the local editor did. Later, my predictions came true, probably gaining the United States more brownie points with this group of German listeners, long after I had left their city. When I rode the train back to Essen late that night, I felt elated. I might have taken a stupid risk by agreeing to the debate, but I had managed to defend my country and my president, the very president I had often criticized for his economic and fiscal policies.

Unusual Encounters on the Language Bridge

Translators and interpreters form the bridge between different languages and different cultures. For the translator, the daily encounters on the language bridge tend to be primarily with the ideas contained in the documents, with dictionaries, reference works, computer software, the Internet, and other translators. For the interpreter, the daily encounters are primarily with people, not only the people he or she interprets for but with many other persons on the interpreting scene or in the path of constant travel. Some of those unusual or surprising encounters leave an indelible record in the interpreter's memory.

This chapter recounts a few of the stories that interpreters will tell to each other or to their friends. Many of them disappear after a few years of oral repetition because they are rarely recorded on paper.

WHERE IS FATHER SCHNEIDER?

April 23, 1967, was a sad day in German history, but a glorious spring sun was shining down on Cologne while the nation was laying its first postwar chancellor to rest. Konrad Adenauer, elected in 1949 at age seventy-three and serving as the leader of the free part of Germany until the age of eighty-seven, had earned the respect of many other leaders. Seated in Cologne Cathedral for his final requiem were Lyndon Johnson, Charles De Gaulle, Harold Wilson, and many other notables.

After President Johnson had decided that he would attend this state funeral, he recalled the German chancellor's visit to his ranch in Texas one weekend. Adenauer had inquired whether he could go to a Catholic mass on Sunday morning, being firmly ensconced in Protestant territory at the ranch. LBJ made arrangements to take him to a small parish on the other side of the Pedernales River, where a German immigrant priest, Father Schneider, attended to a small flock.

Adenauer had enjoyed this Sunday visit, and it had been a memorable day for Father Schneider.

Johnson turned to one of his assistants and ordered him to make arrangements to take Father Schneider along to Cologne on *Air Force One*. But the priest refused to go without first having his bishop's blessing. Getting this done took too long to have him join us in Washington for our departure to Bonn from Andrews Air Force Base. He followed many hours later on the military plane of the chairman of the Joint Chiefs of Staff, who was also flying to Germany.

From the cathedral, our solemn procession followed Adenauer's coffin on foot to the nearby bank of the Rhine, where a boat was to take him to his birthplace of Rhöndorf, a few miles up the river, to be interred there. A few minutes later, I found myself standing near the boat to the right of LBJ, with his bodyguard standing to his left. Behind us were German President Heinrich Lübke and Chancellor Kiesinger, to my right Prime Minister Wilson and President De Gaulle. Many hundreds were gathered behind us in silence.

The German navy detachment had some problem getting the coffin on the boat in a dignified manner. This led to a pause in the procedure before trumpet flourishes could send him off in style. At this solemn moment in German history, Johnson turned to his bodyguard and asked with the firm voice of a commander-in-chief, "Where is Father Schneider?"

The bodyguard got on his walkie-talkie. In five seconds, a Secret Service voice told him, "Father Schneider is 150 feet behind you, holding a Bible under his arm, looking across the river."

The bodyguard turned to me and said, "Please go and fetch him. I cannot leave the president." The priest was easy to find. I firmly took the hand that did not hold the Bible and told him to follow me to our leader.

We arrived in front of LBJ. He briefly greeted the priest, turned around, and said to President Lübke in his Texas drawl and with a warm smile, "Mr. President, I would like you to meet Father Schneider from across the Pedernales River, who said mass for Chancellor Adenauer when he visited me at my ranch."

As Lübke did not speak English, I had to translate this for him. The German president was visibly annoyed. This was no time for social small talk. He gave Father Schneider a pained smile and silently stared ahead at the coffin, which still had not been moved. Realizing that he was at the wrong address with the dour Lübke, LBJ turned to

Kiesinger and repeated, "Mr. Chancellor, I would like you to meet Father Schneider ..."

Kiesinger, a suave diplomat and seeing that the ceremony was still stalled, greeted the priest warmly and had a brief conversation in German with him.

Next, LBJ turned to Harold Wilson and introduced Father Schneider to him. Wilson shook his hand and the priest started to talk to him in German. I whispered in his ear, "Speak English. He speaks English."

Schneider switched to English while I was contemplating how this little affair would go over with Charles De Gaulle, who likely would be next. I was rescued from this dreaded scenario by the sudden movement of the coffin toward the boat while the trumpeters were raising their instruments in preparation for the flourishes. Wilson straightened up and silence ensued, except for Father Schneider asking me softly, "Who is he?"

I replied, "The prime minister of England."

"No kidding!" Father Schneider exclaimed in a voice loud enough to be heard around us, much to the delight of Johnson and the dismay of Lübke. The trumpets began to sound their tribute, bringing an end to this brief encounter between two cultures.

A few hours later, I found myself in Chancellor Kiesinger's office for a "one-on-one".

We were sitting at a table, President Johnson to my right, the chancellor across from LBJ, and German interpreter Küsterer across from me.

At one point, Kiesinger asked LBJ a fairly complicated question about NATO missile defenses. The president seemed at a loss for an answer and wrinkled his brow. Sensing that Johnson needed a few seconds for a reply, the chancellor told him that he had been up since very early, greeting scores of visitors arriving for the funeral. Could he be excused for a brief trip to the restroom? Johnson nodded, and the interpreter, seeing his own rare opportunity, disappeared with his chancellor.

We were alone. The president turned to me and asked, "Mr. Interpreter, how shall we answer that?" Luckily, I had read and half memorized the military part of the briefing book for this meeting. I suggested an answer, and gave him the facts, numbers, and names of weapons. The chancellor returned. Johnson repeated what I had just told him, without missing a beat.

Kiesinger nodded approvingly and said, "Mr. President, I did not know that you are such a military expert." While I kept a poker face, Johnson's left hand squeezed my right thigh, a big Texan thank-you under the table.

THE IMMOVABLE MADAME MITTERAND

President George Herbert Walker Bush and Barbara Bush were giving a state dinner in honor of French President Mitterrand and his wife. For such dinners, the ladies usually wear long evening gowns and their best jewelry. In the White House, they tend to put the finishing touches on their appearance in the upstairs living quarters. Then, at the arms of their husbands, they descend the stairs and pose on the landing for a contingent of photographers. At such photo opportunities, interpreters have to keep their distance.

Alec Toumayan, the American interpreter for the evening, was watching the scene from below and behind the photographers. When the pictures had been taken, President Bush signaled to Madame Mitterrand to take the lead down the stairs. She did not budge. "Please, go ahead!" the president urged gallantly. The French First Lady said something to him in French that he did not understand, but she would not move. Again, the president asked her to go ahead. Still not moving, she repeated what she had said to him in French, this time a little louder, so that the interpreter downstairs could understand it.

Alec cupped his hands in front of his mouth and shouted up to the landing, "Mr. President, you are standing on my dress!"

JUANITA'S PLACE

I was escorting a German politician in a rental car from San Francisco to Sausalito and then on to the Napa Valley. He annoyed me a little because he constantly kept staring at the map of California that I had given him rather than looking at the sites we were passing. When we were returning from our outing in the afternoon, driving south back to San Francisco, he urged me to cut across the hills to a parallel road running south closer to the coast. I reluctantly complied with the request of my navigator. Suddenly, he announced that he needed a cup of strong coffee, "right now, not later." Maybe the glass of wine we had over lunch in Sonoma had made him a little sleepy.

My eyes were roaming both sides of the road, looking for an establishment that might serve coffee. There was nothing in the next ten miles or so. My visitor was getting irritable, as if this was my fault. Finally, I spotted an entrance to what looked like a hotel or restaurant called Juanita's Place.

I made a right turn and followed the driveway toward a small building. To our right were a few small cottages inside the complex, maybe designed for honeymooners, to our left a large open area filled with bathtubs of all shapes and sizes. When we reached the building, I saw an enormous front porch, on which three women were sitting in rocking chairs. One had a monkey on her shoulder, one a parrot, and the third a cat in her lap. My first thought was that maybe the building was an insane asylum. My second thought was that we were in California near San Francisco, and I should not be or act surprised.

One of the women was Hispanic. Maybe that was Juanita. I parked the car, marched up the steps onto the porch, and asked her if the establishment served coffee. "Of course, we do," she replied. "Just walk through the door behind me." We opened the door to discover our second surprise. We entered a large room with an enormous bar seating a dozen or more, though at this moment the bartender was the only person in the room. The entire wall behind the bar was covered with a huge enlargement of an old photo showing the former casino in Santa Cruz. The barkeeper, a young black man, was dressed as elegantly as if he were serving drinks at a Ritz Carlton. His speech and aristocratic demeanor mirrored his attire.

"Good afternoon, gentlemen! What can I serve you?" I explained that we were just passing by and in need of some coffee.

"How do you like your coffee? I shall brew it fresh for you." I glanced around the room, which also contained a pool table and a beautiful jukebox. To the right, a door opened to a small restaurant, which was also empty. While he was making the coffee, I asked him why there were so many bathtubs sitting out in the open. "Juanita collects bathtubs," was his laconic answer.

While we were sipping our coffee, I introduced my visitor. The bartender proceeded to ask him some intelligent questions about Berlin and the life in a divided nation. When we were ready to leave, I asked for the check. He stretched himself up to his full height and said somewhat disdainfully, "Juanita never charges for coffee." We walked out between the ladies back to our car. They just quietly rocked and smiled benevolently. Only the monkey was cackling. We must have seemed awfully weird to him.

FOR INSTANCE, HITLER

During the Nixon administration, I had escorted two prominent Austrian cabinet members on their trips around the United States and had repeatedly gone to Vienna for important interpreting missions. One day, much to my surprise, I was notified that the Austrian president had awarded me a high civilian decoration, the Grand Decoration of Merit. It was an Austrian diplomatic custom that in other countries, this award had to be given to the honoree by the Austrian ambassador as the personal representative of the president. The Department of State gave me its approval to accept this medal from a foreign government.

However, in the fall of 1972, the position of ambassador in Washington had not been filled for a number of weeks. My award ceremony had to await the arrival of a new appointee. In October, a new ambassador, Dr. Gerd Halusa, arrived and my award ceremony became one of his first duties. The invitation first came to me in a telephone call from the embassy's press secretary, who expressed his surprise that I should receive this medal at my early age of forty.

So, on the assigned date, my wife Elnina and I went to the Austrian embassy. At that time, it was still located in a mansion on Massachusetts Avenue (later, the Austrians built a larger embassy in the diplomatic enclave off Connecticut Avenue).

A small crowd of Washington-area Austrians and embassy employees had assembled in the upstairs reception room. Champagne and coffee were served. Finally, the new ambassador entered the room. He was a friendly-looking person with curly hair and big glasses. He also seemed a little shy and unsure how to proceed. My wife and I were asked to stand in front of him. The deputy chief of mission stood to his left and held the presidential proclamation and the medal case in his hands. The ambassador knew little about me beyond that I was the senior interpreter for German for the American government.

His hands folded in front of him, he began a little speech in German. Being the honoree, I did not interpret it to my wife, who understood no German. He began by telling a couple of stories about bad experiences he had had with interpreters. When the second story was finished, the deputy whispered in his ear, "You need to say something positive about interpreting."

The ambassador nodded approval and continued as follows: "Every once in a while, an interpreter comes along who is way above average." He suddenly perked up and thrust his right hand into the air. "For instance, Hitler had such an interpreter, Paul Schmidt." Then he began to extol the virtues of Schmidt. I was biting my lower lip, trying to keep a straight face. My wife, born in New York State, threw a questioning glance at me, because she had understood the mention of Hitler and wondered how that might relate to me, a German immigrant.

The deputy chief of mission put the proclamation in his ambassador's hand in a successful attempt to bring the speech to a quick end. Halusa read the proclamation and handed me the medal. To the relief of the embassy personnel, the ceremony was over, except for congratulations and champagne.

WELCOME TO ARIZONA, SENATOR!

One spring, when it was still very cold in Chicago, I was escorting a senator from Berlin around the United States. He was an accomplished speaker and easy to interpret for. He was also my age and an avid outdoorsman, who loved to hike and swim and dive off the ten-meter board. For a number of days, we had been running around Washington and Chicago in our dark suits and ties, shivering and hurrying from one appointment to another.

During our last breakfast in Chicago, both of us were in our business suits, as we had one more morning appointment downtown before flying on to Phoenix. I told him that the temperature in Phoenix was in the high seventies, that our hotel there had a large swimming pool, and that we could be in the water by late afternoon. He was ecstatic. At 11:30, he came down to the hotel lobby with his suitcase, ready for the ride to O'Hare. Unlike me, still in my business suit, he had already changed into a short-sleeve sports shirt and blazer, chomping at the bit for warmer weather.

As our plane descended into Sky Harbor Airport, we were alerted that we should disembark first because a greeting party was waiting for us on the tarmac. The plane taxied to the spot from where the passengers had to walk into the terminal. When the door opened to a sunny and balmy afternoon, I saw two distinguished gentlemen waiting for us at the bottom of the stairs. I let the senator descend first but stayed close behind him so I would be able to hear and interpret the greetings.

The two greeters walked right past him. One of them rushed up to me, grabbed my hand, and proclaimed, "Welcome to Arizona, Senator! I am the mayor of Phoenix and this is the president of the Arizona Senate. Did you have a good flight from Chicago? I hear it was snowing there."

The German senator got a big kick out of this mix-up, standing with his arms folded and grinning from ear to ear. His demeanor made the mayor angry. He spun around and bellowed at the senator, "Don't just stand there! Would you please interpret what I just said?"

TWO NEAR-DEATH EXPERIENCES AT SHEA STADIUM

In April 1971, I was escorting a group of young Austrian parliamentarians around the United States. Some of them would rise to the top of their country's political establishment many years later: Erwin Lanc would become foreign minister; Erhard Busek, head of the Austrian Peoples party and vice chancellor; Wolfgang Schüssel head of the same party and chancellor from 2000 until 2007.

It was an exciting trip for this talented group, circling along the coasts (Atlantic, Gulf of Mexico, Pacific) and visiting the heartland. There were many surprises. For instance, we arrived in Lincoln, Nebraska, on a very balmy spring evening, having come out of California in our short-sleeve shirts. The next morning, everybody showed up in their California attire for the first appointment to find snow on the ground and a temperature of 26 degrees. Overnight, the temperature had dropped over thirty degrees.

Ten days later, we were at our last stop, New York City. The weather was fine on Easter Sunday. Four of the group wanted to see a baseball game at Shea Stadium, and one wanted to go to the New York City Opera that night to see a performance of *Don Rodrigo* by the Argentine composer Alberto Ginastera. As he also wanted an interpreter along, I went to Shea Stadium in my dark blue pinstripe suit and tie, because there would be no time to change after the game.

The five of us were seated in a lower box, surrounded by a steel railing. Three young men from the Bronx were seated in the box to our right. Explaining American baseball in German to Austrians is a formidable chore for the interpreter. How does one say *bunt, home plate, home run, popup* in German? Worse, the game was a pitching duel. Many of the actions I had described to the visitors never happened in the game. It was a drag. The game must also have been boring to the three raucous young men in the box next to us. They had already consumed a quantity of beer. When they heard German spoken in our box, they started taunting us. They would get out of their seats, turn to us with hands raised in the Nazi salute, and yell "Heil Hitler!" This did not go over well with the Austrians, as one of them had lost a family member in a concentration camp. The burly Tyrolean congressman in our group started to shout back at them and to make threatening gestures. My own diplomatic efforts fell on deaf ears.

Fearing that a brawl might break out, I left the box and went to an usher, several rows up, pleading with him to have us or them reseated. It was too late. When I turned my head, I saw two of the Bronx punks running up the aisle. The third one lay back in his seat, blue in the face, two big Tyrolean thumbs having reduced his collar size to near zero. Adrenalin rushed through my body. My brain imagined a New York headline on Monday, "Austrian congressman kills fan at Shea Stadium." My body jumped down over sets of rails to reach the box before it was too late. I yelled at the Austrian to let go. He was in such a rage that he did not even hear me. The people around us were egging him on, having seen and heard what the Bronx gang had done. The Tyrolean's face was red. The young man's face was white and blue. He had not drawn a breath in a long time. I dug two fingers of each hand under the avenger's thumbs. It took all of my strength to pry them open. The limp hooligan drew a deep breath that you could hear twenty seats away. When his strength returned, he also ran up the aisle to the deck above us.

My back to the game, I was standing in front of my visitors, as we discussed the situation amongst us. It might be best to leave, as our party was not without guilt in the dispute. Suddenly, I received a tremendous blow to the top of my head that dropped me to my knees. I struggled not to pass out and reached for my head. A thick liquid ran down my face, and I could not see anything. Panic struck me. Was this part of my brain? Having escaped death many times before, was I to die in a baseball stadium? My hands reached farther up. My thick Prussian skull had not split open. My Austrian friends helped me up and wiped the liquid off my face. It was liquid soap.

We were sitting just off the edge of the deck above us. The hooligans had dismantled two liquid soap containers in the men's room and dropped them on us from above. One hit me squarely on the head, the other hit the trench coat of a parliamentarian. When we had determined that I did not have a bad concussion, we left for the subway and our hotel. I did not want to deal with stadium security, because the culprits had already escaped and I was worried the Tyrolean visitor might get arrested. My pinstriped suit was ruined. I had to throw it out. The only dark-blue item left was a big bump on my head. My entire bathroom was filled to the ceiling with soap bubbles when I tried to rinse myself off in the shower.

Many months later, I was in Vienna on an interpreting mission. Erhard Busek and two of his colleagues treated me to a dinner at the Weisser Rauchfangkehrer, one of the best restaurants in town. There was no shortage of stories to tell, as we reminisced about their long American journey.

The name of the restaurant illustrates a considerable difficulty that interpreters working between German and English face: the many differences between Austrian German and the German spoken in Germany. The Austrian word for chimney sweep is *Rauchfangkehrer,* but in Germany the occupation is called *Schornsteinfeger.* If you want whipped cream on your cake, you order *Schlagobers* in Vienna, but *Schlagsahne* in Berlin. If you cannot tolerate the strong black coffee in Vienna, you order a *gestreckter Schwarzer* (a "stretched black one"). In Berlin, nobody would know what you are talking about. The names for January and February are different in Austria and in Germany. The interpreter must constantly be aware of what country he or she is in at the time.

HEINRICH AND HAVLICEK

In 1973, I toured the country with a conservative politician from Germany. Heinrich Köppler was a quiet and courteous man, a pious Catholic from the Rhineland. His dress and gait were solidly conservative. As it was early spring, he wore a black overcoat and dark suit and tie every day. When walking with him, I always had to put on the brakes. He walked in slow measured paces, like a bishop walking down the aisle in church. In the many meetings I interpreted for him, he spoke at a deliberate and measured pace, making my job easy.

On Friday, March 27, we were in Atlanta, returning from a morning meeting at the Chamber of Commerce to our hotel. Our taxi passed the Atlanta basketball arena. A sign announced that the Boston Celtics were playing there the same night. Suddenly, my visitor got excited. "I am a great fan of the Celtics," he told me. "Let us go and see the game tonight." How I had misjudged him. There was an entirely different side to his persona.

I ordered the taxi to stop and paid the driver. When we came to the ticket window, there was a sign: "Game Sold Out." It was the last game of the season between two outstanding teams. Köppler was deeply disappointed. I told him I would try to get him a ticket somehow. On the way back to the hotel, he told me about Jo Jo White, John Havlicek, and Dave Cowens. These names meant little to me, as I was a baseball fan. But he seemed to know every player on the Celtics team.

I called the president of the Chamber of Commerce and my other few contacts in Atlanta, pleading for help. They called around to their contacts and friends. Nobody could find us a ticket. Heinrich Köppler sank into depression. I realized that this was more important to him than getting a meeting with the president in the Oval Office. Everything else having failed, we went to the arena forty minutes before tipoff, hoping to find a scalper who had a ticket to sell.

Finally, it was fifteen minutes to game time. Nobody offered a ticket to sell.

I told Köppler to wait for me near one of the gates and walked up to one of the ushers and asked, "Who is in charge of issuing press passes?" He gave me the name. His office was inside the arena. I told him I needed to see him, flashing my State Department badge at him. He told me that that was not a press credential and would not let me pass. I took off my Swiss wristwatch and handed it to him. "I am not trying to get into the game," I said. "Just hold on to my watch for fifteen minutes until I get back." It was an expensive-looking watch. He took it and let me pass.

The man in charge of the passes sat in his office, both feet on his desk, eating chicken and French fries. I pleaded my case for the important visitor from Germany who the government in Washington had made my responsibility. My career may be finished if I could not get him to see the Atlanta Hawks. It was probably not my pleading but the intervention of Köppler's guardian angel at this critical point in the visitor's life. He pulled two press passes out of his desk drawer and handed them to me. "If you are his escort, you should go with him," he said. "I am out of seats in the press box, but I will put up two folding chairs for you at the sideline."

I rushed back out, reclaimed my watch, and found my visitor. He was ecstatic. We were seated just three or four feet from the playing surface, near one of the baskets. A Celtics player lost his balance and crashed across the sideline to the right of Köppler's chair. The visitor spun around to me and exclaimed, *"Aufregend!"* ("Exciting!"). He had become a totally different person. The Celtics won the game 117–110. We had over two weeks left in our trip. Miami, New Orleans, the Grand Canyon, Salt Lake City, Chicago, New York lay still ahead. But nothing was going to top this moment for my visitor. He had seen the Boston Celtics play. What a story to tell after his return to Germany.

MEETING BILL CLINTON

In 1979, I was taking a group of Austrians to Little Rock, Arkansas. Among our appointments was one with the new governor of the state, William Jefferson Clinton. I had never even heard the name before, nor did I know anything about him. Early in the morning, I received a telephone call at our hotel. The governor had a sudden scheduling conflict and would be unable to see us.

That night, a local host took us across the river to a restaurant that served fried catfish and all kinds of beer. None of the Austrians had ever eaten catfish before. They were pleasantly surprised that such an ugly-looking creature could taste so good. We were deep into the fish and on our second beer when the manager told me that he had just received a telephone call from the governor's staff. The governor was on his way to the restaurant to greet the Austrian visitors that he had missed out on in the morning.

After a few minutes, the manager waved to me to come to the front door. When I got there, a baby-faced young man with curly black hair had just come in. He looked the part of a governor's aide, so I walked up to him and told him that I was the interpreter of the group. I asked, "Is the governor outside, or is he still on his way?" The young man grinned, stretched out his hand, and replied, "I am the governor of Arkansas."

He laughed off my apology and came back to our table. The Austrians were as surprised as I had been when I introduced him. The manager brought an extra chair and the governor's favorite beer. He stayed almost an hour to chat with the visitors. They were greatly impressed that he had made the effort to come to see them in order to make up for the missed appointment and by his charm, intelligence, and knowledge of Europe.

Fifteen years would pass until I would sit next to Bill Clinton again. This time it was in the Oval Office for a meeting with German opposition leader Oskar Lafontaine, which I was interpreting. The smiling baby face and the contagious charm were still there, but the black curls were gone.

A TRANSLATOR'S ENCOUNTER WITH HIMSELF

In my early years working for Language Services at the State Department, I was occasionally given some difficult documents to translate into German. Although I had been hired as an interpreter, the circumstance that I had a degree in translation from Mainz University and the most recent exposure to modern German of any of the staff linguists made me a logical choice whenever I was not busy with interpreting.

At that time, in order to bolster its revenue, the federal government was trying to sell uranium enrichment services to friendly European countries. A very technical sales brochure had been written and translated in Europe into a few languages, including German. The finished German translation had been shown to a German-speaking nuclear expert, who declared it full of mistakes and inaccuracies. The text was rushed to Washington just four days before the printing deadline. If the government missed the deadline, it would have to pay a considerable penalty stipulated in the printing contract.

On Friday morning, Theodore Leon, then the head of Language Services, called me to his office and ordered me to put all other work aside and fix the German in that booklet. After reading through it, I decided that retranslating it from scratch would be a better option than trying to correct the many mistakes that could be found on every page. "How many hours would that take?" Forty to sixty hours was my estimate. Leon authorized overtime for the entire weekend, and I went to work immediately.

Although I was somewhat knowledgeable in the field of nuclear fission, I had never read anything on enrichment services, neither in English nor in German. I had a nuclear glossary to work with but could not find anything on the subject in German. Some of the technical terms did not have German equivalents as yet, as none of the German-speaking countries were engaged in that activity.

Having a deadline to meet, I invented a number of German technical terms. For instance, I wrote *Fallprobe* for *falling stream sampler* and came up with a few other new terms. Whenever I did that, I made a footnote with the original English term at the bottom of the page, so experts could trace the meaning to the original. I worked deep into the night Friday and Saturday. On Sunday around midnight, the translation was finished and so were my mind and body.

About twenty years later, I was the director of the Office of Language Services, sitting in my spacious office on the second floor, just off the main entrance of the State Department. One of our staff translators, Emil Fossan, came in to ask my advice. He was translating a paper dealing with uranium enrichment. As usual, Fossan had everything under control except for three German terms he could not identify the meaning of, including an abbreviation: "350,000 TAE." Although I had not dealt with the subject in many years, I remembered two of the terms and was able to give him the proper English equivalents.

However, "TAE" meant nothing to me. I told him I would think about it. Maybe it was hidden somewhere in the recesses of my distant memory.

Before I go on with this story, I have to introduce you to Emil Fossan, a considerably more talented linguist than I ever was, maybe more knowledgeable than any other linguist of his time in the entire United States of America. Emil was born in Minnesota, the descendant of a seafaring Norwegian family. He loved languages and had the ability to soak them up like a sponge.

In 1942, he had traveled to Washington to take a language competency test with the federal government. To the amazement of his examiners, he scored 98 out of the maximum 100 points in all four languages he was tested in: German, French, Italian, and Spanish. The War Department, as the Department of Defense was then called, offered him a job as staff translator. In 1947, The State Department, always in search of top interpreting and translating talent, brought him on our staff. He stayed with us until his retirement in 1984.

Once on our staff, Fossan never stopped learning more languages. His ability to acquire them with great speed was mind-boggling. Apart from languages, his only other passions were baseball and, during his vacations, going fishing in the lakes of Minnesota with his brothers. He never got married. His money went into books and dictionaries, hundreds and hundreds of them.

LS director Obst speaks about the career of former LS staff translator Emil Fossan (seated), who is about to receive the "Linguist of the Century" award at the bicentennial celebration of the Office of Language Services in 1990. In the rear stand chief of protocol Joseph Reed (left) and acting secretary of State Lawrence Eagleburger. *private photo*

By the time he left government service at age seventy-seven, he was able to translate texts from twenty-seven languages into English, including treaties and complicated technical agreements. He was the only translator on our staff who could handle Latin, Sanskrit, Indonesian, Malay, Flemish, Icelandic, Faroese, Danish, Serbian, Croatian, Finnish, Hungarian, and Romanian. He also could help our translators with the Slavic languages. He had a good command of all of them. Yet Fossan was a quiet, unassuming person. He often was overlooked at promotion time and had never received a bonus or award for his enormous contributions to two important federal agencies. As the new head of Language Services at the time of his retirement, I discovered this to my dismay when I called up his personnel file. I wanted to give him a financial bonus, but federal rules did not allow this, because his retirement papers had already been signed and approved.

We finally atoned for this omission six years later. 1990 was the bicentennial of the creation of Language Services by Thomas Jefferson. We created a new award, "Linguist of the Century," and brought him from Minnesota to our bicentennial celebration in the ornate Benjamin Franklin Room. Acting Secretary of State Larry Eagleburger presented him with the award to thunderous applause from the big crowd. Finally, Emil Fossan had received his due.

Now back to our story. 350,000 TAE? What could it mean? I turned this question over in my mind the morning after Fossan had come to my office. My mind usually works best when I am shaving in the morning and there is nothing in the mirror in front of me but my own face, nothing to distract me. With a number in front of the acronym, it probably referred to a measurement. Measurements in uranium enrichment? Suddenly, a distant bell rang in my memory:

Trennarbeitseinheiten was one of those long German words that I had invented twenty years earlier, this one as the translation for *separative work units*. My own baby had grown up and come back to me, and I did not recognize it. It had become a standard acronym in the German technical language.

Fossan was chuckling when I brought him his solution and told him the story. "I have had to invent a few words myself," he said. "That is why dictionaries keep getting bigger."

THE LURE OF THE VIENNA WALTZ

One day, in the mid-eighties, I was in Vienna with Secretary of State George Shultz and his wife O'Bie. At that time, Fred Sinowatz was chancellor and Helene von Damm was our ambassador to Austria. Helene, born in Austria, had been Ronald Reagan's personal secretary for many years when he was governor of California. In Washington, she had been in charge of White House personnel until she was sent to Vienna as our ambassador.

One afternoon, Chancellor Sinowatz held an afternoon reception for Shultz in a big ornate reception room. Coffee, tea, wine, and champagne were served. Because Mrs. Shultz was present, the Austrian dignitaries had also brought their wives along. Maybe to facilitate the men talking business and the women socializing, the women were seated at small tables at one end of the hall and the men at the other end. It reminded me of the dance halls in the Scottish highlands. In the middle, there was a sort of demilitarized zone, occupied only by an orchestra playing

Viennese waltzes. The polished hardwood floor was ideal for dancing, but everybody was just sitting and talking.

I was interpreting between the secretary and the chancellor at our separate small table, where Helene was also seated as the only woman in the male zone, so the secretary could have his ambassador by his side. Sinowatz, not known for great charm and diplomatic skills, carried on a somewhat lackluster conversation with his guest while the orchestra was beguiling the secretary with vivacious waltzes. Getting a little impatient, Shultz said to Sinowatz, "I have always wanted to dance a waltz in Vienna." A seasoned diplomat would have interpreted this not as a hint but as a demand to be granted at all costs.

To my surprise, neither the chancellor nor the ambassador, herself an attractive woman, picked up on this. Instead, they started another lackluster subject. There are times when the interpreter has to step out of his subservient role and become an icebreaker in an awkward situation. This seemed to be such a situation.

At this moment, Thomas Klestil and his wife entered the reception room. Klestil was at that time the Austrian ambassador in Washington (he later was to become president of Austria). Always an accomplished diplomat, Klestil, before escorting his spouse across the DMZ to the women's tables, stopped by to greet Shultz and his chancellor. While he was speaking to Shultz in English, I pulled Mrs. Klestil aside and whispered to her, "Mr. Shultz very much wants to dance this waltz with somebody." Without a moment's hesitation, she handed her purse to her husband, pulled the secretary out of his chair, and asked him to dance with her. They whirled across the dance floor with some flair, as Shultz had no trouble mastering a waltz. He was beaming with delight, a few other men rushed across the DMZ for their mates, and dancing was finally under way. After the dance with the ambassador's wife, the secretary found O'Bie on the other side of the hall and had another waltz with her. He was finally enjoying this reception.

TRAINING INTERPRETERS IN THE UNITED STATES

DECADES OF NEGLECT AND INACTION

The accurate and complete consecutive interpretation of a long spoken passage by a master of the profession takes his or her mind to its outer limits. It combines knowledge, experience, multitiered analysis, and creativity in a process similar in nature to composing a symphony, building a bridge across treacherous waters, or plotting a flight path to the moon. It is a great art, and that art has had a home at the universities of many countries in the twentieth century and beyond, even though the emphasis of the curriculum has shifted more to simultaneous interpreting methods in recent years, due to the rapidly rising demand for simultaneous interpreters by large international organizations like the European Union.

When you hire an interpreter in the United States, you will often get a bilingual person, not a skilled professional. When you hire an interpreter in Europe, you will get a highly trained professional, nine out of ten times.

At many universities in such countries as Belgium, Canada, Finland, France, Germany, Russia, and others, professional interpreters and translators are routinely trained alongside physicians, architects, engineers, and lawyers. This process reaps considerable benefits for those societies in many areas of human discourse, especially in the fields of international relations and in the selling of goods and services to countries where different languages are spoken.

But the training of professional interpreters has never found a home at the universities in the United States of America. Here, the dominance of theoretical linguists in key positions has always pushed aside the applied language arts. The United States has a long and unfortunate tradition of making do with untrained interpreters. Their widespread presence and substandard job performance creates a false image of the nature of the art. At most of our universities, there still exists a profound ignorance of the intellectual challenges presented by reliable interpretation and translation. University decision makers do not understand that these professions demand the same depth of knowledge, sophisticated methodology, and intellectual acumen as most of the other professions that have a home in academia.

It is fairly easy for deans and university administrators to fashion programs for teaching foreign languages or theoretical linguistics. Even though the quality of foreign language training leaves much to be desired at many of our universities and colleges, teachers are easy to find at a moderate cost, while good teachers for interpretation and translation cost more and are harder to find in this country, the latter, again, a product of the absence of good training facilities and of a sufficient number of seasoned professionals.

The training of interpreters in the United States at all levels, not only the master level, is a wasteland; more than that, it is a national disgrace. The neglect of academia, the absence of meaningful state or federal initiatives, except for the area of court interpreting, is a sad disservice to a great nation.

A meeting to design an interpreter training course at the Department of State in Washington. From left: staff interpreter Dr. William Hopkins, LS director Obst, and staff interpreter Dimitri Zarechnak. *private photo*

In her autobiography *Madame Secretary*, the former secretary of state Madeleine Albright states, "Interpreters play a vital but overlooked part in diplomacy. The best ones are able to translate not only words but also points of emphasis and tone, and are careful to ensure that idiomatic expressions are not misunderstood."

"Without our translators [interpreters], we are deaf and dumb," a Marine captain fighting in Iraq testified during an immigration hearing on Capitol Hill in 2007. After the terrorist attacks on September 11, 2001, the FBI director pleaded on national television for help. The FBI needed Arabic-language speakers, interpreters, and translators, but could not find them in the wealthiest nation on earth, with many hundreds of universities and colleges. The U.S. Army had to institute its own crash program to train interpreters in the middle of the Iraq War, because it had no private or public training institutions to go to in the United States that could have trained a large number, reliably and quickly. So important were the interpreters to the military effort that many hundreds of additional untrained interpreters had to be recruited from the Iraqi population, just anybody who could speak English and at least one of the local languages. The few combat units working with skilled and trained interpreters were the lucky ones. They could obtain accurate information in search-and-rescue operations and during interrogations. By 2008, over 250 trained and untrained interpreters had lost their lives in the war, according to a report in the *Washington Post* on January 22, 2008.

You would think that fact might prompt journalists to try and understand the difference between interpreters, who deal mainly with the spoken word, and translators, who almost exclusively translate written documents. Reflecting the general ignorance of the public about these two professions, many journalists and even TV news anchors cannot distinguish between the two and constantly mix them up. On February 29, 2008, veteran staff writer Walter Pincus wrote an article for the *Washington Post* entitled "Visas for war zone translators halted." He meant interpreters, of course, but the word *interpreter* does not appear once in the entire article.

The American business community also needs reliable interpreters and translators just as badly as the armed forces. Strangely enough, the average corporation is not even aware of this. You conquer shares of foreign markets much more easily if you have employees and managers who are fluent in the foreign language. The managers who are monolingual are a less likely to be successful in selling American goods and services to non-English-speaking countries if they do not have recourse to professional interpreters and translators of their own.

Toyota, for example, has conquered a large share of our automobile market and is now beginning to surpass some of our carmakers in sales in our own country. It may soon trump General Motors and become the largest carmaker in the world. It already has more than 40,000 employees in the United States. How did Toyota get there? It all started with sending employees and managers over here who spoke our language. If not, they brought interpreters with them. You cannot quickly survey a new market in a country where your native tongue is not spoken if you do not have good language tools to work with. American managers could not walk into Japanese law libraries and get a feel for the local rules and regulations for conducting business. The Japanese were able to do that here and read our trade publications with reasonably good understanding of their contents.

As early as the 1960s, when there were already 10,000 Japanese sales agents in the United States, only a few dozen Americans with knowledge of Japanese were looking for business opportunities on the other side of the Pacific. Today, Toyota and other Asian corporations are very much at home in our country. They have built large manufacturing and distribution facilities here. These doors to our markets were opened in many areas by skillfully using the language key. Every Toyota factory in the United States has professional interpreters and translators on their payroll. In our business enterprises, they are still a rarity. Only a few corporations, Microsoft, for instance, have smartly used professional linguists to conquer large slices of foreign markets.

More than twenty years ago, I paid a visit to the language services unit of Siemens Corporation in the Alpine region of Germany. There I found a highly professional outfit of about two hundred company translators and interpreters who knew the company philosophy, modus operandi, and technical terminology inside out. They were equipped with the most modern tools of the trade, including a self-generated machine translation system for the limited and very basic translation chores that such a machine can handle. At that time, Siemens was bidding to sell telephone switching systems in Latin America. The company even brought retired telephone engineers from the targeted countries to Germany to assist their linguists with getting the technical local Spanish exactly right. This is how you use language tools to conquer foreign markets. Siemens won several contracts in Latin America with the aid of this effort.

We are the largest national economy in the world. Our workers are extremely productive. Yet year after year, we are losing a greater share of our domestic market to foreign corporations than we are able to recoup in exchange overseas. As a result, we are constantly running enormous trade deficits that keep widening and will not go away. We need to learn from the foreign countries how to open new markets through the use of skilled linguists. A significant portion of our trade deficit would disappear if we had a sufficient number of foreign language speakers and, for the more difficult tasks, trained professional interpreters and translators.

When will the American business community wake up to this? It is in its interest to lean heavily on our universities, to demand and help to fund training facilities for those indispensable professionals. We are not going to sell goods and services overseas with people who have studied theoretical linguistics, of whom we have an overabundance. American universities find teachers, funding, and classrooms for them by the thousands. But they refuse to train a few hundred professional interpreters and translators. Over a span of several decades, our academic institutions have not bothered to seriously analyze, determine, and quantify our society's need for professional interpreters and translators and the size of the benefits the nation can obtain from sound training programs. The universities in most other advanced countries have done so. Their societies are reaping the considerable benefits of this research and the accompanying academic training effort. Maybe a big carrot and a big stick from the business community would produce some stir in the American Ivory Tower.

American programs that did exist, such as a well-established program at Georgetown University in the District of Columbia and a sound fledgling program at George Mason University in Virginia, were abandoned years ago. Today, I can only name one small university in California—the Monterey Institute of International Studies with its Graduate School of Translation and Interpretation—that teaches the art as it should be taught and offers a master's degree in interpretation for several foreign languages, including the major Asian languages that are of growing importance today.

For thirteen years, when I was the director of the Office of Language Services at the Department of State, an institution employing hundreds of interpreters, I made the rounds of American universities, pleading for programs to train interpreters. It was like pleading with the Taliban to give university training to women. Virtually nobody wanted to listen, and nobody started a meaningful and comprehensive program.

One day, I sat at a table at Georgetown University with the director of its moribund interpreting school, Dr. Margareta Bowen, a highly skilled master-level interpreter herself, and with the dean of the School of Languages and Linguistics, which the interpreter training program was part of. I had come there to offer the university a government grant to train Russian language interpreters for the State Department. The dean was visibly disappointed when he heard that the grant was for the small interpreting program, which was of little interest to him. To the consternation of Dr. Bowen, he fell asleep in the middle of my presentation, the ultimate body language. I gave the small grant to the interpreting program in Monterey instead. This incident was typical of the lack of interest by university decision makers in this field, many of them coming out of programs dealing with theoretical linguistics, with little knowledge of applied language skills. Quite a few of them consider interpreters and translators as belonging to inferior occupations, not worthy of academic training. They are not impressed by the fact that their colleagues in other countries totally disagree with them. Knowledge is trumped by hubris and disinterest.

There is only one area of training professional interpreters in the United States where some meaningful progress has been made over the last twenty years: the training of court interpreters. As a result of some terrible mistakes and misjudgments made in hearings and trials in state and federal courts that were traced to incompetent interpretation, states like California, New Jersey, and New York early on led the way to establish interpreting aptitude tests and certification. By now, there is even a common consortium test that is valid in more than half of the states, which did not honor each other's certification before.

There is also a cumbersome certification procedure for federal courts, though most of the non-Spanish-speaking federal court interpreters are still uncertified today. Because passing the test and winning certification has now become essential in most states for the successful pursuit of a career as a professional court interpreter, a modest number of training programs were established. Even though in most of them the emphasis is on court terminology and court procedures rather than on sound interpreting methodology, the quality of court interpreting is improving consistently. Even where skilled teachers for consecutive interpretation are not available in such programs, drilling the students in simultaneous interpretation, a technique used more and more in the courts to save time, is very helpful.

A very small number of these courses have recently found their way into colleges and universities, even though limited to court interpreting only, and frequently limited to the Spanish-English combination, where the demand is the greatest. It is my hope that this trend can be a Trojan horse through which more comprehensive interpreter training will sneak its way onto some university campuses. Similar fledgling initiatives have been under way recently in the area of medical interpreting, the fastest-growing interpreting specialty since the 1990s. Here again, the absence of trained interpreters and the mistakes of the amateurs, to the detriment of patients and physicians, have finally prompted long overdue action in testing and basic training.

The above-cited areas of progress represent only a few watering holes in the vast desert of neglect. In addition, many teachers in existing programs are linguists or language teachers by training, not interpreters. Unfamiliar with sound interpreting techniques, their courses are heavy on teaching terminology, ethics, and conduct. Yet the interpreters coming out of those programs usually can deliver statements with poise and will use correct terminology. This clearly represents progress. But they still often cannot capture the correct meaning of what was said, and they cannot retain longer passages. They must work sentence by sentence and suffer from the stress of having to take interpreting notes in longhand, because they were never taught the proper use of ideograms and memory-enhancing notation structure, as described earlier. Nor do they usually receive useful memory training.

The author (at that time the director of the Inlingua School of Interpretation in Arlington, Virginia) with his class of interpreting students in Ulaanbaatar, Mongolia in 2000. *private photo*

I have personally tried to make a modest contribution as a teacher of professional interpretation. When working as a staff interpreter at the Department of State in the 1970s and 1980s, I frequently volunteered to give in-house interpreter training for department contract interpreters, who number over one thousand. Faced with having to train interpreters whose languages I do not speak, I developed methods of omnilingual (language-neutral) training that worked quite well and allowed me to train interpreters in Chinese, Japanese, Vietnamese, and Turkish, for instance.

From 1997 to 2004, I was the principal instructor at the former Inlingua School of Interpretation in Arlington, Virginia, teaching beginners the basic methods. My associate teacher was Laszlo Szimonisz, a highly skilled diplomatic interpreter with command of Hungarian, German, Turkish, and English. Laszlo has also interpreted for several American presidents. That program has also disappeared. Our courses concentrated on the proper methodology of accurate consecutive interpretation, memory training, and professional note-taking techniques. Students do not need much help from the instructor with the provision of terminology. During the daily interpreting exercises, it suffices to point out what is obviously not correct. The needed terms can be looked up by the students in dictionaries and on the Internet, and learned by heart. The teachers should not waste much time on providing such terminology. One hour of methodology is worth five hours of terminology.

In addition, technical and common daily terminology changes every few years. What you learned five or ten years ago is suddenly useless. *Underdeveloped countries, developing countries, less developed countries* all mean the same thing. As each new label becomes acceptable and fashionable, interpreters had to drop the term they had learned before. They must keep up with the times and cannot rely on what they learned in class. The eternal problem for interpreters is, of course, that they must store the acquired words in their memory, as they cannot use dictionaries in the act of performing their service.

With that in mind, Laszlo and I left the acquisition of terminology largely to our students to save time for the more important teaching tasks. Many of them do well in the journeyman ranks of the profession today. Even their limited basic training puts them two steps ahead of their many colleagues who never had any meaningful instruction anywhere.

Retired professional interpreters make ideal teachers of the art. But somebody has to give them an institution at which to teach. The leading university schools of interpretation in the world make a point of having a cadre of professional interpreters among their faculty.

It takes five million dollars to train one aircraft carrier pilot. Nobody has ever seriously argued against spending this money. It is in the national interest. Trained professional interpreters are also in the national interest. You can train a large number of interpreters for five million dollars. One properly trained diplomatic interpreter's skilled translation may avoid the conflict in which that carrier may have to be used, at a possible cost in the tens or hundreds of millions. Yet billion-dollar universities will not spend a few hundred thousand dollars, let alone a few million, to create viable training programs for interpreters and translators. Let them look at the cost of their schools of medicine or their schools of law. Much less money is needed for this important effort, which any society needs in times of war as in times of peace.

It is my hope that our business community and our military leadership will soon demand professional training schools for American interpreters and translators, and supplement the academic effort with funds of their own. The federal government and our state governments should help in this effort. Relative to the benefits obtained, the cost of such training is negligible. This also provides well-paying jobs for young Americans.

A good professional interpreter makes considerably more money than a good language teacher.

We have shown that we can train reliable carrier pilots who do not miss the deck and run their planes into the ocean. Though prohibitively expensive, that money is well spent. We should also be able to train reliable interpreters and translators at a fraction of that cost, so they can build the golden bridges for diplomatic initiatives and business ventures in other countries, provide non-English speakers with proper medical care, and offer a fair hearing and due process in our courts.

Biographical Data

1932	born in Konigsberg, East Prussia, Germany
1949	escapes from communist East Germany
1949-50	coal miner in Essen, West Germany
1954	high school diploma in Essen-Werden
1954-56	studies languages, translation, law
1956	graduates from Mainz University
1957	emigrates to the United States
1957-65	marketing and management positions in private industry
1963	becomes American citizen
1965-84	Diplomatic Interpreter, U.S. Department of State, Washington, interprets for seven American presidents through 1996
1970-2008	lectures in Europe on the U.S. political, economic, and cultural scene; lectures and gives seminars on interpretation in the U.S. and Europe
1972	awarded the Grand Decoration of Merit by President Jonas of Austria
1973	German President Heinemann invites Obst to Berlin for a private discussion of the American cultural and political scene
1984-97	Director, Office of Language Services, U.S. Department of State in Washington, occasional White House interpreting by name request
1997	retires as member of the Senior Executive Service with merit awards from Secretary of State Madeleine Albright and USIA Director Duffey
1997-2004	Director and principal instructor, Inlingua School of Interpretation
1999-2000	gives interpreter training courses in Ulaan Baatar, Mongolia
2004-2010	writes and lectures in retirement